MICHAEL FASSBENDER

THE BIOGRAPHY

MICHAEL FASSBENDER

THE BIOGRAPHY

JIM MALONEY

JOHN BLAKE

Published by John Blake Publishing Ltd,
3 Bramber Court, 2 Bramber Road,
London W14 9PB, England

www.johnblakepublishing.co.uk

www.facebook.com/Johnblakepub   facebook

twitter.com/johnblakepub   twitter

First published in hardback in 2012

ISBN: 9781857828047

British Library Cataloguing-in-Publication Data:

A catalogue record for this book is available from the British Library.

Design by www.envydesign.co.uk

Printed and bound by CPI Group
(UK) Ltd, Croydon, CR0 4YY

1 3 5 7 9 10 8 6 4 2

Papers used by John Blake Publishing are natural, recyclable products
made from wood grown in sustainable forests. The manufacturing
processes conform to the environmental regulations
of the country of origin.

CONTENTS

INTRODUCTION

As a child, Michael Fassbender believed he could fly. In fact, he was convinced that he was Superman and he still remembers his joy at being bought a Man of Steel outfit when he was six.

Such childhood beliefs and imaginings are not uncommon but few of us grow up and still play superheroes and villains. Even daydreaming Michael, growing up in the countryside of Killarney, could hardly have believed that one day he would become steel-bending X-Man Magneto. But then, his belief in himself has always been strong, despite his parents' worries about him at school and his lack of direction. However, once he had found his way – by chance – he set about it with an enviable and unwavering determination.

His rise to stardom may seem meteoric but it only went into hyper-drive following his breakthrough movie *Hunger* and by that stage he had put in plenty of groundwork. Having quit drama college early after becoming disillusioned with the way they did things, he set about getting an agent and, with the impetuousness of youth, felt that he was ready to make his mark. But it very nearly cost him dearly as he missed out on the college's auditions process and he spent years in the wilderness, scrapping for acting jobs which were few and far between. To support himself he worked behind bars in London, barely able to afford the living standards of the capital. Memories of these days are never far from his mind and, even today, he respects bartenders and is appreciative of a well-stocked and well-run bar!

Back then his goal in life was to earn a living solely as an actor. That achievement took some time – a lot longer than he had imagined – but it was an invaluable experience that gave him the time to learn his craft, make some mistakes, come to terms with them and move on, and to appreciate the good times when they finally came. It has helped to keep him grounded amid the glitter and showbiz razzmatazz of premieres, parties, awards and a fan base that continues to expand.

Hollywood royalty such as George Clooney, Brad Pitt and Quentin Tarantino are now among his friends. But he remains firm to his roots and strives to return home to see his family and friends in Killarney at least three times a year. He remains very close to his parents and has enjoyed the opportunity of being able to take them to showbiz premieres and awards gatherings. And they are very proud of their famous son as well as their academic daughter.

Michael has mixed with some of the biggest names in the business. He's been acclaimed at glitzy awards ceremonies for his acting, shared a drink in Venice with Tarantino, joked with Brad Pitt and danced with Keira Knightley. But one of the most enjoyable things he has done in his life – since he became a star – was something he had dreamed about as a teenager. Michael and his father Josef had talked back then about one day taking a road trip through Europe on motorbikes. At the time he had neither a bike nor a licence but, as he has a habit of doing, he eventually made the dream come true. They had the most marvellous time and it was a life-enhancing experience that neither of them will ever forget.

Once he'd got his break with *Hunger*, Michael made a string of films at a hectic rate, forcing himself into public consciousness. Another dream of his had been to find a director with whom he could bond and work with on a regular basis and he found that in Londoner Steve McQueen, who first directed him in *Hunger* and then in *Shame* – both of which received huge acclaim. Neither movie was easy, to say the least. To play Bobby Sands in *Hunger* he went on a strict diet to lose over two stone and in *Shame* he had to undergo full-frontal nudity and sex scenes to play a sex addict.

Michael has a chameleon-like ability to lose himself and take on the personas of the various roles he is playing. He might be a star but there is an everyman quality to him that allows audiences to forget the actor and really believe and engage in whichever character he is playing. As Steve McQueen put it, 'Apart from being big and strong and bold, there is a fragility to Michael, and certain things are revealed through him that we can see in ourselves, and that's very rare. He has a heart. You're never disconnected from him.'

Michael is also always challenging himself. While some stars are concerned about their image and in taking on the right roles to fit their public persona, Michael firmly rejects such behaviour. If the script and character interest and intrigue him, he will take it on. Nothing else matters. Along the way, he has played a wife-beater, a serial murderer with a foot fetish, a devil, a psychotic killer, a paedophile and an assassin – and he has spanked Keira Knightley!

Despite having joined the A-list, Michael still feels an outsider in Hollywood but that has as much to do with his upbringing as anything. A curious mix of Irish and German, his name stood out at school when the family moved from Germany to Killarney when he was two. At home Adele insisted that he speak German at the dinner table so that he would be bilingual and there is certainly something of a dual personality about him that fits the stereotypes from both countries – a steely Germanic discipline on the one hand

and a cheerful, rousing partygoer on the other. 'I don't feel hugely nationalistic, whether it be Irish or German or anything,' he says. 'So I guess what my background gave me is the idea that the world is so small that borders seem a bit absurd.'

It's all part of the mix in Michael's everyman quality that makes him so interesting. His belief and confidence in himself overlap with an innate shyness. He also has a nice modesty about him but also a genuine fondness for people. He happily signs autographs for fans, poses for their pictures and chats with them whenever he is approached and it's all done with his trademark wide grin. It's the smile that makes many women go weak at the knees. And then there's the piercing blue eyes, the soft Irish accent, the toned physique. But he's no pretty boy – he's very much a man's man with rugged good looks. Red-blooded males see him as a down-to-earth type who's one of the lads – someone who you could have a drink with, share a laugh or play sports with.

Michael has brought that same naturalistic quality to his acting. He's been feted as the next Brando, the next Pacino, the next Daniel Day-Lewis – all of whom were teenage heroes of his. Every role he takes on is given a hundred per cent. His preparation is intense and has often astounded his fellow actors and directors. He strives to really get under the skin of his characters, to play them for real. Even a comic-book character such as Magneto in *The X-Men: First Class* is treated in the same way. Michael gave the character gravitas and filled him with conflicting emotions and an inner turmoil that had audiences caring about him. He wasn't simply just good or bad.

Variety has always been the spice of life for Michael. A string of work in British TV dramas eventually led to *Hunger* and he has not stopped taking risks since. 'He's the real deal,' says Gary Oldman.

Michael has the ability to play independent movies one moment and studio blockbusters the next. And he doesn't always need to be the star. Often he takes subsidiary roles that interest him. In Steven Soderbergh's *Haywire*, he only made a relatively brief appearance with its star Gina Carano but it was the most memorable scene in the movie. Similarly in Quentin Tarantino's war movie, *Inglourious Basterds*, he had little screen time but played the part of British officer Archie Hicox to perfection, culminating in an unforgettable Mexican stand-off with Nazi officer Major Hellstrom in a French bistro, where both men are holding pistols under the table aimed at each other's crotches.

Michael has appreciated the kindness and encouragement that he has received from some of the biggest names in Hollywood and, in turn, he has tried to help and encourage others trying to make it in the business. Straight after filming the big-budget *Inglourious Basterds*, Michael returned to London to film a short called *Man on a Motorcycle*, made on a shoestring by former musician and video-maker John Maclean, who was making his film debut. Michael had admired his videos and offered to appear in any film he made. John hurriedly wrote one and, true to his word, Michael fitted it into his hectic schedule of back-to-back movies.

From a sexual predator amid the council homes of Essex in the low-budget *Fish Tank* to the romantic Rochester in *Jane Eyre*; from a muscular Roman soldier in *Centurion* to a humanoid in the space fantasy *Prometheus*; from a sex addict in *Shame* to sex therapist in *A Dangerous Method* – there seems to be nothing Michael is not capable of doing. In the main he has shown a knack for choosing excellent roles. No one gets it right every time but, even in those films that have failed to set the world alight, he has usually been praised for his own performance. Along the way he has collected numerous Best Actor awards from around the world – many for his portrayal of Brandon in the uncompromising *Shame*. His full-frontal nudity in this movie made him the butt of much good-natured ribbing from family and friends in Ireland to Hollywood stars George Clooney and Charlize Theron.

The exciting thing is that Michael is still a young man and this is just the beginning. As he says, he likes to keep people guessing about what he will do next. 'I've been going on my gut pretty much from the beginning. I'm not always going to get it right but risk interests me. There is some embarrassing element to everything I do in life. I used to beat myself up a lot but, if you're really going to learn and expand, you're going to be open to doing things that perhaps don't work out the way you envisaged. I'm not going to hamper myself with fear.' But he takes every day as it comes, enjoying the moment and appreciating his good fortune, and doesn't fret about what he should or should not be doing. 'I don't say, 'I have to play the Dane [Hamlet] one day,' he says. 'I don't really think like that. I just wait and see what comes up and I'm always open to it. If I react to the script, I'm up for anything.'

It was Michael's mother, Adele – a big fan of American cinema from the 1970s – who instilled in him his love for movies and first brought to his attention the talent of the character actor John Cazale who played, among others, Fredo Corleone in *The Godfather*. Cazale has remained one of Michael's heroes, along with the likes of Marlon Brando, Robert De Niro, Al Pacino, Gene Hackman, Robert Mitchum, Montgomery Clift, Daniel Day-Lewis, Sean Penn and Paddy Considine.

Another man he calls one of his heroes is Steve McQueen and he will remain forever grateful to the director for the 'lucky break' that turned Michael from a jobbing actor into an international name and set him on the course to stardom. 'Steve is family to me now,' he said. 'We're so close on and off set. He changed my life, giving me the opportunity in *Hunger*. We were heading into a recession and there were fewer roles for fewer actors. For me, a thirty-year-old unknown, to get a leading role, and somebody willing to take a risk – that was a big deal, which allowed me to show potential within the craft. I'm forever indebted.'

CHAPTER ONE

BOY FROM KILLARNEY... VIA HEIDELBERG

Michael Fassbender stood out from the crowd while he was still at school but this had nothing to do with star appeal or talent. It was because, in a classroom full of O'Sullivans, Kellys, Murphys and O'Connells, his unusual surname at first raised eyebrows among teachers and gave way to some gentle mickey-taking from fellow pupils. His name has continued to intrigue ever since, from casting directors to interviewers. A German Irishman? An interesting mix. 'I suppose the German side wants to keep everything in control and the Irish side wants to wreak havoc,' he was later to joke. But he wasn't being just frivolous with this remark because it does help to explain the two contrasting sides to his character: Michael the focused, methodical, confident actor, and Michael the easy-going, free-wheelin' charmer.

He was born in the city of Heidelberg in south-west Germany to a German father, Josef, and an Irish mother, Adele. Heidelberg is a city where a pretty Old Town of cafes, shops and restaurants co-exists with a bustling modern business centre and technology park, with an emphasis on science and research. Nestled in the hills of the Odenwald along the banks of the Neckar river, it boasts a castle and the oldest university in Germany. Students, businessmen, scientists and tourists are all attracted to the city, which has something to offer to all of them.

Josef Fassbender was a successful, hardworking local chef who had worked in various hotels in Germany, Spain and England, including London's famous Savoy. It was in a London nightclub that he met Adele, who had grown up in Country Antrim, Northern Ireland. They began going on dates together and, as their romance blossomed, they eventually married and she moved with him to Heidelberg, where he continued to work as a chef. But Adele missed Ireland and after starting a family she persuaded Josef of the benefits of bringing up their children in the countryside, suggesting that southern Ireland would be ideal and that he could get plenty of work there. So it was that in 1979 they moved to Dromin, Fossa, in Killarney, County Kerry, on the south-west coast of Ireland, with their two children, Catherine and two-year-old toddler Michael.

Fossa is located on the shores of Lough Léin, in the shade of the McGillycuddy Reeks four miles west of

Killarney town. The talented Josef became a chef in Killarney's luxurious German-owned Hotel Europe and later Head Chef at the elegant Hotel Dunloe Castle. Although Adele came from Larne, Country Antrim, her family, generations back, were from the south and family lore has it that she is the great great-niece of the Irish revolutionary hero Michael Collins. As Michael was later to say, 'We're only going by my grandfather's word but I believe it.'

Michael's maternal great-grandfather was disowned by the family after he joined the Royal Irish Constabulary and moved to the North. He returned years later hoping to be reconciled with his family but they still wanted nothing to do with him.

With Adele's relatives still living in Northern Ireland, the family would often visit during summer holidays and at Christmas, and Michael remembers how very different things were once they had crossed the border. British army patrols checked cars going in and out during The Troubles and they would have to get out of their car while soldiers searched through the seats and boot for possible guns, ammunition or bomb-making materials.

In the early years in Fossa, when pre-school Michael was four and five years old, he felt a little lonely as all the other boys in his immediate neighbourhood seemed to be three or four years older than he was, so he spent a lot of time on his own and would retreat into a world of his own imaginings.

Adele, who spoke fluent German, insisted they talk it at the dinner table, which Michael found embarrassing as he got older, but it taught him the language and was to be instrumental in launching him to stardom when he auditioned for Quentin Tarantino. But even the daydreaming young Michael never fantasised that he would become a Hollywood star. His thoughts were firmly set on becoming a superhero!

It was when this rather insular, shy young boy started attending the local primary school, a short walk from his home, that he came out of his shell and learned to integrate with children of his own age. The principal of Fossa National School was the former Kerry Gaelic footballer, Tom Long. The 149 boy and girl pupils dressed smartly in a uniform of burgundy jumper, cream shirt, grey trousers/skirts and striped ties. To this day, Michael has many happy memories of his time there. 'The Irish education system is really top notch,' he was later to say. 'At primary school I learned about the battle of Thermopylae and 300 Spartans when I was six or seven years old. There was a real love of learning language and poetry, and we were taught history and geography. It was very well rounded.'

The Battle of Thermopylae took place in 480 BC in ancient Greece, when King Leonidas of Sparta and 1,400 men (700 Thespians, 400 Thebans and the King's bodyguard of 300 Spartans) bravely defended the pass of Thermopylae to the death against a much greater force of invading Persians.

This knowledge was to come in useful many years later when he found himself portraying a Spartan warrior caught up in the famous conflict in the movie *300*.

Despite his grounded education, Michael still had his head in the clouds and when on his own he enjoyed daydreaming and fantasising of heroic adventures far from Killarney. Such was the strength of his imagination that when he was six years old he was convinced that he was a young Superman. At night in bed he would hear a buzzing in his ear and thought it was Kryptonite calling him to the garage – although he wasn't sufficiently fearless to get up to investigate! Michael was delighted when his parents bought him a Superman outfit. Now there was no stopping him. They could hardly get him to take it off and had to put up with him leaping and jumping heroically around the house. And all this really made his flying take off – or so he thought.

'I would practise leaping off the couch and when my sister came in I'd say, "Look, look, I've flown a little further!"' he remembers. 'I wanted to take it [the outfit] to the swimming pool so I could practise my flying but my parents wouldn't let me.' And what he couldn't do for real he recreated in the finest traditions of stage and cinema trickery. 'I used to play this game with my cousin where he would dress up in civilian clothes – like Clark Kent – and he would stand by the side of the road and when a car came he would run behind a bush and I would come out from the bush dressed as Superman.'

Michael has described these childhood years as 'living in little pockets of fantasy' – flying a spaceship, climbing trees and pretending to be the *Six Million Dollar Man* or the *Fall Guy*, two of his favourite TV shows, starring Lee Majors. Irish television imported a lot of American shows like this – *CHiPs, Magnum P.I., The A-Team, Knightrider* – and they were firm favourites with Michael and many other children. Michael had an uncanny knack of being able to reproduce a very accurate impression of each show's theme tune, making guitar sounds and drumbeats with his mouth. It's something that he can still do and which he describes as being almost OCD [obsessive compulsive disorder]. Among his party pieces these days are the remarkably realistic bird-calls that he learned as a child, the sound of a motorbike or a Formula 1 racing car and the beeping of a pedestrian crossing signal!

In particular Michael loved Tom Selleck, who played *Magnum*, a private investigator living on Oahu, Hawaii, with a penchant for colourful Hawaiian shirts and shorts. And Michael yearned to grow a bushy moustache like his when he got older! 'I loved Tom Selleck. He did such a great job on *Magnum P.I.*,' he recalled. 'I don't think many men can carry off wearing shorts like that!' Oddly, his childhood knowledge of the show was also to resonate with Tarantino years later.

Inspired by such TV shows, the historical stories at school and the beautiful Killarney countryside, Michael would take himself off for hours at a time, sometimes playing with friends he had made at school, at other times alone. His parents felt that Killarney was a safe place for him to explore and play and, as long as he was back home for dinner at 5.30pm, they encouraged him to enjoy the outdoor life.

One film he was desperate to see was *Jaws*. His parents told him he would have nightmares about man-eating sharks if he did but they relented when his grandmother persuaded them that he would be fine. He should have listened to his mum and dad. The night after watching it he laid in bed, feeling very frightened and vulnerable, and fearing that a huge shark was lurking in the shadows below him.

Another film he really wanted to see was based on the comic-book adventure *Flash Gordon*. He was very excited when Josef took him and his sister Catherine to the local cinema in Killarney. But such was its popularity that they had to join a long queue and, despite waiting what seemed like an age to get in, they were turned away after the cinema became full to capacity. Michael can clearly remember his disappointment to this day. Another letdown came after they got a VCR for their home and bought a videotape of *ET*. Michael and Catherine were terribly excited and could hardly wait for their dad to put it on. Poor Josef then had to tell them that the tape was incompatible with their player.

One day at school, when he was six, he had a little 'accident' in the classroom. There was a rule that pupils were only able to use the toilet at lunch break or at the end of the day. Michael was unable to contain himself and a little puddle started to form underneath his chair. 'I think the teacher was more embarrassed than I was,' he remembers. But one thing that did embarrass him was public speaking. Never one for reading – unlike the studious Catherine – the quiet and shy young Michael felt terribly self-conscious whenever he was asked to read aloud at school. But at home he was much bolder and less inhibited and, as his hero worship of Superman gave way to that of Michael Jackson, he would try to copy his dancing whenever he heard his music or watched him on television.

'It was a happy childhood, for sure,' he recalled. 'Killarney is such a beautiful place. What's special about Ireland is that we are steeped in storytelling, whether it's poems, songs or novels. To have that rich involvement in the arts has influenced me. I guess that's why I do what I do.'

His secondary school was St Brendan's College, situated near St Mary's Cathedral and close to Killarney's National Park. The impressive grey stone building with arched windows was initially built as a seminary where students were prepared for ordination as priests. Founded by the Bishop of Kerry, David Moriarty, it opened its doors on 16 May 1860, on the Feast of St Brendan, and was known then as the Bishop's New Palace and later St Brendan's Seminary. Bishop Moriarty and two priests lived in the upper part of the building and students were taught downstairs. Over the decades, the building grew in size as more classrooms, a science lab, showers and toilets were added and it became a mainstream school with a uniform of blue shirt, tie, navy jumper and grey trousers. Sport was an important aspect at the college, particularly Gaelic Football, and many former students have gone on to sporting glory. Up until the late 1960s the college was mainly staffed by diocesan clergy, with a priest acting as President and school principal, but gradually lay teachers took over these roles. By the 1970s its official title had become St Brendan's College but it is still widely known as 'the Sem' by teachers, students and locals.

Just as he'd had to do at primary school, Michael frequently had to explain his surname. Fassbender translates as 'cooper', Fass meaning 'barrel' and bender the person who made the barrels. But kids being kids, they were not interested in such humdrum explanations and took great delight in calling Michael 'Slowbender'.

After hearing from the parish priest, Father Galvin, that the spirit of God was always right next to them, Michael would make room for the spirit in his bed at night. 'I'd make room for the teddy bears, Jesus and me,' he smiled. At the age of 12 he became an altar boy and was given the responsibility of holding the keys to the church, which he had to open in the morning and lock at night. On a couple of occasions he overslept and, in a panic, rushed across fields to the church to find the whole congregation waiting to be let in.

Michael was later to liken performing in a solemn Catholic church ceremony – mass, baptism or funeral – at the altar to being on stage. 'The suspension of reality – the idea that wine turns into blood and bread turns into flesh – was a very visceral thing to deal with, and the ritual and theatre of it.' But, he always wondered, why did he need to go to a priest for confession? If God was always by his side, why couldn't he communicate directly with him?

As a shy 12-year-old, Michael's pastimes included making a bamboo bow and whittling tree branches into arrows for archery. He had a natural musical ear and learned to play the guitar and the accordion. Each week he attended Fossa Youth Club and joined in when some of them entertained local senior citizens, playing the accordion and being part of the dance team.

Josef was keen that his son should work hard at school and Michael remembers him as being difficult to please. 'If I came home with eighty per cent in a test, he'd ask, "What about the other twenty?" My dad drove it home to me that, if you're going to do something, do it properly.' This has certainly been his approach to acting. His intense preparation for each role would often amaze his co-actors and directors.

Adele also inadvertently helped to shape her son's future career. She had a passion for arts and loved movies. The German film director Rainer Werner Fassbinder –

known as the 'enfant terrible' of the New German Cinema during the 1960s and 1970s for his provoking and often disturbing films – was one of her favourites. Although he was no relation to Josef Fassbender – and the spelling is different – Michael always joked that the similarity of names was one of the reasons why his mother had married Josef.

Adele was particularly fond of 1970s American cinema. Her favourite actor was John Cazale, who played Fredo Corleone in *The Godfather* and Sal in *Dog Day Afternoon*. Sadly he died of cancer in 1978 at the age of 42, having made just five feature films. They are all widely regarded as classics, however, the other three being *The Conversation*, *The Godfather: Part II* and his final film, *The Deer Hunter*.

Michael became as big a fan of Cazale as his mother, along with the stylish yet naturalistic crime films of the era, including *Mean Streets*, *Serpico* and *Taxi Driver*. 'It was a golden era and Cazale didn't put a foot wrong with his movie choices,' Michael once explained. 'He played unappealing, cowardly, sickly characters. He was very good at releasing any ego and bringing these characters to a very real space without making them very clichéd.' Cazale would be a big influence when Michael turned to acting. Other actors he admired included Marlon Brando, Robert De Niro, Al Pacino, Gene Hackman, Sean Penn, Robert Mitchum and Montgomery Clift.

As the awkward adolescent years kicked in, *Magnum*

P.I. was usurped as his favourite TV show by *Wonder Woman*. This starred Lynda Carter as a sexy superhero who would quickly change into her skimpy outfit of tight, cleavage-enhancing bodice, pants and knee-high boots, via the aid of TV visual effects of super-fast revolutions and a flash of light. 'I was always trying to capture her between the change,' Michael recalled. 'I felt unusual things were happening to me and I didn't understand. Cartoons might be on the other channel but I no longer wanted to watch them.'

He remembers, too, the excruciating experience of Josef sitting him down and giving him the 'sex talk'. 'I was like, "Oh God, why does he have to do it?" I think I was thirteen and I had a girlfriend. It was embarrassing as hell, like "Urgh!" I knew about all that anyway – you know, boys at school, who'd picked it up from older brothers and cousins.'

Adele, who enjoyed singing around the house, encouraged Michael's musical talents. In traditional Irish fashion he started by playing the tin whistle and then progressed to the piano accordion. He really wanted to play the violin but his parents told him that violins would be too expensive to buy. Later, like many teens the world over, he picked up a guitar and dreamed of being in a band. In Michael's case, it was to be the lead singer in a heavy-metal band. He particularly admired Kirk Hammett, lead guitarist with Metallica. But although Michael grew his hair long and was adept at flamboyant rock-star posturing with the guitar in his bedroom, when he heard how good some of his friends were playing the guitar in reality, he knew that he was just not good enough.

It was questionable, too, whether he had the true rock-star temperament. On one occasion he and a group of friends travelled to Dingle where they were going to busk on the streets but they were put off when it started to rain. They persuaded a local publican to let them play inside his pub but heavy-metal music at lunchtime was not of great appeal to his customers and they were repeatedly told to 'turn it down'. Eventually they were playing with unplugged electric guitars before deciding to give it up as a lost cause!

In 1993 Josef and Adele took over a popular restaurant called West End House in the town centre, opposite St Brendan's. Josef worked in the kitchen and established a reputation for excellent but unfussy French bistro food, while Adele was front of house. But the first few years were tough and when Michael asked for trainers and fashionable clothes, he would often be told that they couldn't afford it. It taught him the value of money and of hard work. Nothing comes easy. But Michael and Catherine were somewhat spoiled with the beautiful meals that they got to eat in the restaurant. A particular favourite of Michael's was his father's rack of lamb and even now Michael follows the way Josef taught him to do it. He was later to describe his father as being 'an artist in the kitchen'.

Michael earned pocket money by helping his parents at their restaurant, washing up and waiting on tables. He later remarked that it was good training for an actor being 'front of house' where you need to be smiling and looking happy no matter what turmoil is going on in the kitchen or in your own life. His parents made sure that he put away half the money he earned as an investment for the future.

When he was 16 Josef and Adele let Michael live above West End House during the week in exchange for doing weekend shifts downstairs. The restaurant was three miles from home and he enjoyed the independence this gave him. He spent much of his spare time wandering through the beautiful Killarney National Park, nestled among the mountains, with its acres of woods, lakes and grassland where red deer roam. The area is steeped in history. Here, on the edge of a lake, stands romantic Ross Castle, built by O'Donoghue Mór in the 15th century. It came into the hands of the Earls of Kenmare, who owned an extensive portion of the lands that are now part of the Park, and was the last stronghold in Munster to hold out against Oliver Cromwell's forces, eventually succumbing to General Ludlow in 1652.

Despite Michael's interest in films, he never even thought about acting at that stage. He admits to being an average student with no real idea what he wanted to do with his life – 'pretty clueless and irresponsible'. Unlike his academic sister, Catherine, who loved reading and was always asking questions, he was much more interested in his imaginative world and doing physical things, such as playing in the park and climbing trees. Sometimes he would 'skive off' school with a friend, Ernest Johnson. Whenever Michael got nervous about it, Ernest would take the philosophical approach and ask, 'What'll it matter in a hundred years' time?' This phrase stuck with Michael and whenever he had concerns about taking certain acting roles he would just remember Ernest's words and get on with it. The philosophy also chimes with that of director Steve McQueen, who Michael was to meet some 17 years later – 'We're all going to die anyway, so we might as well just get on with it' – a phrase that Michael has often repeated.

For a time Michael considered a profession in law but, being only an occasional and slow reader, he felt that he would not be able to keep up with the many legal books and documents that he would need to plough through during his studies. Architecture was another idea that evaporated after he failed his technical-drawing exam. His thoughts then turned to journalism and he particularly fancied being a war reporter. He hoped to do well enough at school to be able to go to college in Dublin but fate was to lead him in another direction.

CHAPTER TWO

A FATEFUL DAY

Catherine was now at the prestigious Trinity College in Dublin, studying psychology and neuroscience, but Michael was much more vague about what he wanted to do in life. He was only an average pupil at school and did not have the focus, application or academic ability of his sister. But then one fateful day, when he was 17, he happened to see a piece of paper on the school notice board offering a new Wednesday afternoon activity. The message was from Donie Courtney, a former pupil who had taken a course at the Gaiety School of Acting [the National Theatre School of Ireland] and come back to introduce drama and comedy classes to his old school.

Courtney had set up a couple of workshop classes and an intrigued Michael went along and found that he thoroughly enjoyed the experience. It provided an ideal outlet for his creativity and fantasies and, to his surprise, he did not feel shy or self-conscious when acting. As he was later to explain, 'It just felt right to me, as a way to express myself. All these people in my head could finally find a place to go.'

Disappointed when the classes came to an end, he caught sight of Courtney in town shortly afterwards and, after telling him how much he had enjoyed the acting classes, eagerly asked if there would be any more. Recognising his talent and enthusiasm, Courtney told him about a professional theatre company he had set up in Killarney called Bricriu – named after a troublemaker from the Ulster Cycle of Irish myths and legends – and suggested that he go and do some part-time stuff with them. It was a pivotal moment for Michael – it set him on the course of acting and sparked in him the realisation that it was something he was good at and could possibly do for a living.

'That was it,' he explained. 'It happened fast. I felt it was something that I could really do. It's really thanks to Donie and Bricriu that I got started [in acting]. Donie opened up the whole world to me.'

At the theatre company he did pantomime, theatre in pubs, sketch work and improvisation, keenly absorbing as much as he could about the various techniques. His first performance was on stage in a pub in an off-the-wall production called *Fairytales Fairytales 123* – an amalgamation of *Red Riding Hood, Jack and the Beanstalk* and *Cinderella*. He played one of Cinderella's ugly sisters!

Initially, he wanted to get into comedy movies. He loved the film *Fletch*, starring Chevy Chase as an investigative reporter, and had watched it so many times that he practically knew the script by heart. But his thoughts turned towards drama and, although he enjoyed theatre, it was the world of movies that enchanted him.

'Aside from his looks, he was very talented,' Courtney recalled. 'He had charisma and this drive to succeed. You could see he had huge talent.'

For the first time Michael had a focus on what he really wanted to do with his life and he became a driven man. 'Once I realised perhaps I could be quite good I committed to it a hundred per cent. It was my one and only priority.'

Avidly he studied his favourite actors in his favourite movies – Marlon Brando, Gene Hackman, Robert De Niro, Al Pacino et al., wanting to get to the level they had achieved. He also ploughed through their biographies but it didn't always make for encouraging reading. 'When I read that Pacino and De Niro were nearly thirty years old when they broke through, I remember thinking, "Jesus, will it take that long?"' he recalled.

Quentin Tarantino's stylish gangster movie *Reservoir*

Dogs made a big impact on Michael and his school pals. One afternoon they were re-enacting the chilling scene at the warehouse – in which Mr Blonde cuts off the ear of a policeman to the tune of *Stuck in the Middle With You* – when Michael turned to his friend Marco and said that they should do a stage version of it.

Showing the boldness and confidence of youth, Michael left the Bricriu after less than a year to set up his own production company with his friends. They put on a play version of *Reservoir Dogs* at local nightclub, Ravels, in Killarney for two nights, with Michael producing and directing. He also played the part of Mr Pink, made famous by Steve Buscemi in the film. 'I guess that was the advantage of doing it myself – I got to cast myself in the best part,' he said. 'Mr Pink always appealed to me because he was a survivor, an almost rat-like character – he would survive any sort of outcome. I just thought it was an interesting character to explore. I approached him more like [Robert De Niro's] Johnny Boy in *Mean Streets* than the Buscemi characterisation. Like a loose cannon.

'It went down really well. We had 114 people for the first night, then 140. We packed out the club.' Michael wanted to hand over the door money to a charitable organisation but whenever he mentioned *Reservoir Dogs* he found people backing away, concerned about any association with a film notorious for its violence. In the end he gave the proceeds to some people trying to raise money for a little girl whose sight was impaired and needed an eye operation.

Putting on the production proved to be a wonderful learning experience about the various aspects of performance – acting, producing, directing and publicity. And it gave Michael confidence for the future. 'I was totally naïve but I learned so much,' he said. 'I didn't know what the hell I was doing but I knew that with hard work and enthusiasm, things get done.'

Talking about the production on Radio Kerry he was asked how on earth he had managed to get the rights to put on *Reservoir Dogs*. A nervous Michael just grinned and replied, 'Don't mention that!'

When Michael told his parents that he wanted to act for a living they cautioned him to get a degree first but he insisted that he had to go for it straight away. He was supported by his grandmother, who also felt he should go for it. Not used to such clarity and forcefulness from their dreamer of a son, Josef and Adele eventually let him have his way.

After leaving St Brendan's, Michael worked in his parents' restaurant during the day and acted at night. Josef, who had given his son a strong work ethic, had always instilled in him the idea of 'don't do it unless you're going to do it properly' but he was not enamoured with his son's choice of career and, more than once, told him to 'get a proper job'.

Josef was worried about acting being such an unstable

profession, in which the majority were unemployed and the fact that success depended as much on luck and whom you met as it did on talent. He also didn't want his son to be heartbroken by failing to make it. But seeing that this was no passing phase, and admiring his drive and ambition, he gradually became more supportive. Josef was to later joke, after Michael had made it in Hollywood, that he was pleased his son hadn't listened to him!

After leaving St Brendan's Michael moved to Cork to study drama at the Coláiste Stiofain Naofa [College of Further Education] for a year before progressing, at the age of 19, to the prestigious Central School of Speech and Drama in London, where he enrolled in a three-year course. But money was tight and it didn't go a long way in London. 'It took me a while to come to grips with how expensive London was," Michael told the *Hollywood Reporter*. "My parents helped me out but we never had a lot of money. So it was very sticky the first three or four years between paying drama-school fees and surviving. The first place I lived was a studio I shared with a Brazilian girl. We weren't seeing each other or anything but I remember there was a big hole in the window and it was so cold in the winter.'

Michael found work in a bar at Victoria Station that paid £3.29 an hour. He would do an 11-hour shift on a Saturday and work from 11am-4pm on a Sunday, but he was put on emergency income tax deductions until his correct tax code for the year could be worked out based on his income. This, he said, left him with something like £15 to take home. 'It was a real struggle for the first three years and, to be honest, I don't know how I did it.'

But although he admired and respected his drama teachers, it was not a happy experience for him at the school. He dropped out after two and a half years. 'I'd had enough. You start off with thirty-two students and when I left there [were] eighteen or so remaining because people were getting kicked off or whatever. It was pretty harsh. And they didn't think of movies as a pure art form like theatre acting, but it's films that I love most. There's an intimacy in movies – I wanted to have the same impact on others that movies had on me. So I got an agent and reckoned I had learned as much as I could. But it was a mistake, actually. Nobody knew who I was then for ages because I missed it when all the agents and casting directors came.'

But Michael's naked ambition had its day – after a fashion – when, at the age of 21, he landed a television commercial for Scandinavian Airlines System (SAS). In this cheeky advert Michael plays a young man who wakes up in a strange bed and wonders where he is. Then he turns to see he is lying next to a naked girl and smiles smugly. In need of a drink, he walks downstairs naked, opens the fridge and takes out some milk. Viewers see his bare behind. Suddenly, the light comes on in the kitchen and Michael turns and, to his embarrassment, sees the girl's mother staring at him. A message then comes up on the screen: 'When you'd rather be somewhere else. Inexpensive flights for people under 26.'

Michael had to fight his shyness in having to strip off on screen. It was a daunting prospect for someone who had never been on television before, let alone naked. Despite Sweden's reputation for being more at ease with nudity than many other countries, Michael had expected to be provided with some sort of covering for his private parts. 'But they were like, "OK, when you're ready Michael, drop your boxers and we'll go for real this time." So that was my first screen test and my first job.'

His next job was significantly more highbrow. In May 1999 he joined the Oxford Stage Company's touring production of Chekhov's *Three Sisters*, playing second lieutenant Fedotik. It was an innovative production by the company's talented artistic director, Dominic Dromgoole, which won good reviews. But then... nothing. The phone went quiet and Michael began to regret leaving drama school too early.

He got a job in a factory unloading boxes but the hours meant that he was unable to attend auditions – the lifeblood of the fledgling actor – so he quit that job to do bar work, which was far more flexible. But eight or nine worrying months went by with no acting work forthcoming. Things were looking grim and thoughts of returning home were recurring. Then, quite unexpectedly, he landed a job in what was to become one of the most respected TV series in history, helmed by Hollywood royalty Steven Spielberg and Tom Hanks.

CHAPTER THREE

HOLLYWOOD AND BUST

The 1998 movie *Saving Private Ryan* was a huge hit and earned its director, Steven Spielberg, an Oscar and a nomination for its star Tom Hanks, as Captain John H. Miller, who leads a team of US soldiers in a search to rescue a paratrooper in Normandy, who is the last-surviving brother of four servicemen.

Hanks and Spielberg felt that they could do more in this territory with a TV series and after Hanks read Stephen E Ambrose's true account of 'Easy Company' parachute infantry, he was sure he had found the right story. He and Spielberg approached the US TV company HBO with their idea for a 10-part TV series called *Band of Brothers*, which would follow a US paratrooper unit from their first day of training through to being dropped in Normandy on D-Day 1944 and their eventual capture of Hitler's mountain eyrie at Berchtesgaden.

HBO were extremely keen on the idea, especially because the multi-Oscar-winning duo was behind it, and they backed the project with a hefty $120 million budget, making it the most expensive TV series ever produced. A large ensemble cast of young actors was required to play the soldiers and auditions opened in the US, UK and Australia. Not surprisingly, they attracted hundreds of hopefuls. Michael Fassbender was one of many who went along to audition in a damp basement in London's Soho.

The casting agents at the various auditions were to gradually whittle down those who auditioned for them until they had the required number. Only then would they turn their minds to whom would play who. After having read a trial piece, Michael went back to working in a London bar and it was another month before he heard that he was wanted for a second audition. In the meantime, he had also auditioned for another high-profile role in another WWII adventure – the big-budget Hollywood movie, *Pearl Harbor*.

It told the story of childhood friends, Rafe and Danny, who grew up to become First Lieutenants in the U.S. Army Air Corps. Rafe meets and falls in love with a Navy nurse named Evelyn Johnson but has to leave her behind when he volunteers to serve with the RAF in England. After he is shot down over the English Channel and presumed dead, Danny and Evelyn embark on a relationship. Rafe unexpectedly returns and confronts Danny at his base in Pearl Harbor but when the Japanese launch a surprise attack, the pair have other things on their mind.

It was the first film that Michael had auditioned for and he was sure which role he wanted – the starring one of Captain Rafe McCawley. But he lost out to an actor who was already a star, Ben Affleck, who was cast alongside Josh Hartnett and Kate Beckinsale. The film, made by Jerry Bruckheimer, was distributed by Touchstone Pictures – the film label of the Walt Disney Group – and Michael has never forgotten how nice they were in rejecting him! 'The Disney people were really sweet,' he told the *Hollywood Reporter*. 'They sent me a letter saying that they very much enjoyed the audition and what I did but unfortunately it wasn't going to work out this time. I thought that was really nice of them. They didn't have to do that. You get a lot of letters of rejection but it's not very often you get a nice one that gives you a glow of pleasure!'

Shortly afterwards, to his amazement, he landed the role of Sergeant Pat Christenson in *Band of Brothers*. He was 24 and felt that he stood on the threshold of stardom. 'I felt that this was it. Steven Spielberg. It doesn't get bigger than this,' he recalled. Michael's friend who owned the London bar where he was working cautioned him that, although he was sure that he would do well as an actor, it might take him another five years. But Michael, with his head in the clouds, dismissed his words, telling him he was 'on a roll here' and that he didn't want to hear such things.

The actors were sent to a British Army training centre at Longmoor Camp in Hertfordshire, in the hope of trying to turn them into realistic soldiers. Always one to enjoy physical activity, Michael enjoyed the running, hiking and assault courses. 'After a couple of days the actors thought they were soldiers,' he told the *New York Times*. 'But then we looked across at some real soldiers training a hundred yards away and everyone became an actor again pretty quickly!'

In a largely unknown cast, British actor Damian Lewis was surprised to find himself cast in the lead role of Major Richard Winters and fellow Brit, Dexter Fletcher, played Staff Sergeant John Martin. The few well-known names included Donnie Wahlberg as Second Lieutenant C. Carwood Lipton and David Schwimmer as Captain Herbert Sopel, who puts the rookie soldiers through their arduous training in the first three episodes.

Band of Brothers was shot over eight to ten months at the Hatfield Aerodrome in Hertfordshire, England, where *Saving Private Ryan* had been filmed. Here various sets were constructed to portray 12 different European towns. The picturesque village of Hambleden, in Buckinghamshire, was used for the early scenes where the company are training in England, and other scenes set in Germany and Austria were shot in Switzerland.

The young male cast of ambitious actors, herded

together in an exciting and big new television drama and playing soldiers, created a bond between themselves. There were many laughs during training and most of them, including Michael, couldn't believe their luck. They felt like overgrown children playing a game for which they were being handsomely paid. Michael felt that his days working behind a bar were firmly in the past.

He got on well with Donnie Walhlberg, who paid him a compliment after Michael did a small scene. Donnie approached him and said, 'Well done in that scene. That could've ended up on the cutting room floor and you handled it well.' He then gave Michael some advice he has remembered ever since: 'Just remember the three Ps – patience, perseverance, practice.' Michael appreciated Donnie's words, considering them to be 'a nice bit of encouragement'.

Michael also got to know the Scottish actor James McAvoy, who had a role as Private James Miller. Initially James had thought that Michael was American but after hearing his Irish accent he introduced himself. Michael recalls being impressed by the confidence that James had and liked his sense of mischievousness.

Band of Brothers proved to be a huge hit, winning an Emmy and Golden Globe for best mini-series. On the back of its success, several of the cast – now good friends from the months they had worked together – headed for Los Angeles, where they felt that fame and fortune were waiting for them. Unfortunately it didn't turn out that way. They found themselves competing against each other for the same type of roles, along with many other rising stars. They had been let into Wonderland but once filming had wrapped, they were outside once more, having to knock on doors to be let back in. Although Michael met and had talks with key players in the film world, he failed to get any acting work in the three months he was there.

When the money he had made dried up, he turned to bar work once more, this time in LA, and also got a job unloading trucks at night. But this left him tired when he needed to be fresh during the day for attending auditions. It was Josef who persuaded him to give up the unloading job so that he could get some more sleep.

Michael had thought he had hit the big time with *Band of Brothers* but in LA he realised just how tough the auditioning process was among so many actors, many of whom were far more confident than him. 'I was auditioning for television roles but I made a terrible mess of most of them and I was quite intimidated,' he admitted. 'I felt very embarrassed and eventually went back to London with my tail between my legs.' He returned to working at the same bar, with his friend's earlier warning that it might take five years before he really made it ringing in his ears.

'*Band of Brothers* was an incredible thing to be a part of,' he said, 'but the experience taught me a lesson, to never think you're flying. Once the money had gone, I went back to working behind a bar. It also taught me to keep an eye on your finances because you never know what's around the corner.'

Michael decided that he wouldn't go back to LA until he could sustain a proper acting career. And that was to take longer than he thought. As the months went by without any acting work, turning into a year, his anxiety rose incrementally. He had to think about giving it up and forging another career but the only thing he knew about was catering, so he thought about opening his own bar or returning to Killarney to run his parents restaurant. 'I thought, "Shit, if this [acting] doesn't work, what am I going to do?" I didn't go to university so I don't have anything academic to fall back on. But I do know the world of catering so maybe there was something I could do there.'

For a while he got part-time work doing market research whereby he had to telephone people who had filed complaints about the Royal Mail to see if they were satisfied with how their grievances were dealt with. 'Most of the time they weren't,' he remembered. 'We would do various things to keep our brains from freezing, like trying to stick the words Mary Poppins or another phrase into the conversation.'

Some acting work did begin to come his way but it was sparse and he was later to realise that he probably seemed too desperate during auditions. 'I made a balls of so many auditions. Lost so many jobs.' The constant rejection was 'killing his spirit' but he remembered Donnie Wahlberg's encouragement and advice and tried to convince himself that he would succeed. 'My goal was for acting to become my main income. I would say to myself, "I'm good enough." That became my mantra.'

Bit parts in several British TV drama series followed, including the ITV drama series *Hearts and Bones*, which focused on the lives and loves of a group of female friends who had moved to London from Coventry. Michael appeared in three episodes as a German motorcycle courier, named Hermann, who embarks on a relationship with one of the women, Sinead, played by Rose Keegan. It was good casting because it utilised his knowledge of the German accent and his love of motorbikes as well as his good looks.

Among his other parts was that of a character named Jack Silver in the BBC's stylish cop drama *NCS Manhunt*, starring David Suchet, which was based on the National Crime Squad. But a guest role as a patient named Christian Connolly in the BBC hospital drama series *Holby City* – in a 2002 episode called *Ghosts* – was a miserable experience. 'They were taking my spleen out and I fell asleep,' he remembered. 'I was lying on that bed for six hours. I remember waking up midway through the take and the director saying to the cameraman, "Oh, we'll have better guest actors in the next episode." I thought that was awful. The conveyor belt-ness of it was pretty soul-destroying as it was, without hearing that from the director.'

In the ITV1 one-off drama thriller *Carla*, he had a small role as a man on holiday on a beautiful Greek island, where he catches the eye of two fellow holidaymakers Helen and Carla (Lesley Sharpe and Helen McCrory). Based on the novel *Improvising Carla* by Joanna Hines, the story follows quiet Helen North who arrives on the island, having recently split from her boyfriend, hoping for some peace and quiet during her two-week holiday alone. But then she meets the charismatic Carla whose infectious sense of fun proves irresistible. An intense bond grows between them as they open up to each other about their lives and secrets and fantasies. When they pick up two young men – Rob, played by Michael, and Matt (Henry Ian Cusick) – sexual jealousy rears its head and the trust between the two friends is irrevocably damaged. Carla, it transpires, is not as fun loving and easygoing as she appears. A vicious fight ends with a tragic accident and Helen returns home, shocked and frightened, her dream holiday having turned into a nightmare.

The Times described it as '*Thelma and Louise* with an undertow of *Fatal Attraction*'. The general view is that it looked nice – it was filmed on the lovely Greek island of Kythira – and was well acted but that the plot twisted and turned too much and was ultimately unbelievable. 'The scenery was lovely to look at and the two main characters were superbly cast but there were times when watching olives grow would have been a better way of spending an evening,' said the *Daily Express*. 'Like so many "psychological" thrillers, this one promised more than it delivered,' asserted the *Daily Mail*.

A Radio 4 10-part serialisation of *Dracula*, which was broadcast in the late night *Book at Bedtime* slot between 24 November and 5 December 2003, was very popular with listeners. Michael narrated as Jonathan Harker – the English solicitor who visits the count at his castle and who becomes increasingly horrified by his host and finds it impossible to leave.

The *Observer* newspaper commented, 'Michael Fassbender's Jonathan Harker has the perfect voice for the part – slow to panic – with the result that we do his flapping for him. He soberly described the count crawling down the castle wall like a nightmare lizard. Worse was to follow, of course, starting with the ladies with red lips ready to swig blood. What a nightcap.'

The Times thought it scary enough to keep everyone at wake at night. 'Who was it who decided that the best time to present a dramatised reading of Bram Stoker's *Dracula* should be when any normal person should be looking for a bit of an assist into the arms of Morpheus rather than being wound up into a ball of fear?' it commented, adding, 'A fine cast (including James D'Arcy, Gillian Kearney and Michael Fassbender) gives it plenty of oompty. And consider this – if you tune in every night of the reading, you can stay awake for an entire working week!'

Another unusual job cropped up for Michael in November 2003, as the star of a music video for the British band The Cooper Temple Clause, for their song *Blind Pilots*. He played a man whose fiancé gives him a cowbell necklace to wear as he leaves home on his stag night out with his pals. She warns his friends to look after him but he goes from bad to worse the more he drinks. He starts to become aggressive and then grows horns and turns into a devil-like figure before ending the evening as a fully-fledged goat!

The next job that Michael took to help pay the bills was a TV commercial for Guinness. It seemed to be just another job and not a very dramatically satisfying one at that. But it was to have the most unexpected consequences as it turned him into an overnight star... in Ireland.

CHAPTER FOUR

AN ACTOR'S LIFE

The Guinness advert showed Michael playing a man, seen home alone in Dublin. On the spur of the moment he leaves the house and strides down to the Cliffs of Moher in County Clare, where he dives in and swims, fully-clothed, across the Atlantic. Arriving in America, he walks with determination through New York and into a bar where he confronts a man drinking. The two stare at each other for a moment before the new arrival says, 'Sorry.' There's a tense pause until they smile, embrace each other and enjoy a pint of Guinness together.

The advert, called *The Quarrel*, was first shown on 3 December 2003 and struck a real chord with the public.

After years of acting in various TV dramas, it was this that made him a recognisable face in his homeland.

It was a particularly pleasant job for Michael because he also got to drink a fair bit of the famous product. 'They want you to do as many takes as they can physically get out of you, so by the end I was pretty drunk!' he told Irish chat-show host Ryan Tubridy on *The Late Late Show*. It also opened his eyes to what he thought just might be the best job in the world. 'A guy travels around with them and he pours the perfect pint for the Guinness campaigns,' he said. 'And I thought, "What a brilliant job!" I thought *I* had a brilliant job but that's pretty unique.' Michael cheekily asked if they could give him 'a Guinness credit card' so that he could have free Guinness for the rest of his life but this was declined!

The thought of a swift rise to stardom after the false dawn that was *Band of Brothers* was now a thing of the past but acting work was steadily increasing and Michael, now 26, was becoming a 'jobbing actor'. His next TV role was a high-profile one – that of Guy Fawkes in a BBC2 drama called *Gunpowder, Treason and Plot*, by the acclaimed writer Jimmy McGovern. The two-part story re-told the plot to blow up the Houses of Parliament during the reign of King James I and saw Michael co-starring in a strong cast that included Robert Carlyle as King James, Emilia Fox, Tim McInnerny and Daniela Nardini.

Michael grew a beard and moustache for the role and enjoyed dressing up in a flowing white shirt and tight breeches, and riding a horse. The drama was filmed in Romania and, despite his impressive co-stars, he managed to draw praise from both the critics and the writer. The *Sunday Times* commented, 'Mention should also be made of the devastatingly handsome Michael Fassbender as Guy Fawkes.' *The Observer* said, 'This is drama of the highest order,' and the *Daily Mirror* called it 'a fine drama brimming with passion, hell-fire and damnation'. And Jimmy McGovern, after watching Michael's brooding, cold-hearted and ruthless portrayal of Fawkes, was perhaps the first to say, 'He's the next James Bond.'

Another strong role for Michael was a TV drama called *Julian Fellowes Investigates: A Most Mysterious Murder – The Case of Charles Bravo* in 2004. The interesting pilot for a proposed series, it was such a success that more duly followed. The format had the Oscar-winning *Gosford Park* writer and *Downton Abbey* creator Fellowes introducing a famous real-life murder mystery, which was then dramatised, with Julian cropping up on screen from time to time to narrate details and to invite viewers to play detective and find out 'whodunit'.

Michael played the title role of Charles Bravo, a newly married barrister who died from poisoning in April 1876 in an incident that scandalised Victorian society. It raked up a background of sex, intrigue and jealousy, and the newspapers had a field day. Bravo's wife, Florence, was the wealthy daughter of an Australian millionaire and grew up in a magnificent stately home in Oxfordshire. At the age of

19, she married an MP's son, Alexander Ricardo, and enjoyed a privileged lifestyle inside the coveted circle of high society. But Ricardo was a violent alcoholic who hit Florence. After he died suddenly in 1871, she inherited all he had and embarked on an affair with an eminent doctor, James Gully, who was 40 years her senior. During a house party in 1872, the host returned from a walk unexpectedly to find Florence and Gully having sex on the drawing-room sofa. The story quickly spread around London and Florence was finished in society. There was worse to come. She had fallen pregnant by Gully and he performed an abortion on her.

Desperate to reclaim some of her reputation, Florence lowered her sights to focus on an ambitious young barrister, Charles Bravo. He was beneath her in the social class rankings but was about as good as she could now get in husband material and he was attracted by her fortune as much as her prettiness. When she wanted to keep control of her capital, Bravo threatened not to marry her, so she agreed to give him part of her fortune. Bravo went through with the marriage, even though she had admitted her affair to him and her pregnancy by Gully. But later he became violent, making Florence's life a misery and frightening her and her companion, Mrs Cox.

After Bravo's death, an inquest found that he had been wilfully poisoned but there was insufficient evidence to fix the guilt on any person or persons. Despite the most exhaustive investigations at the time, no one was ever charged with his murder. Fellowes runs through suspects – Florence, Mrs Cox (who may have resented Bravo's treatment of her mistress) and the equerry whom Bravo had fired for insolence and who had vowed to get revenge. At the end of the programme he gives his opinion on who he thinks did it while the audience is left to agree or disagree.

With a regular stream of increasingly good roles coming his way, Michael had the confidence to give up bar work again and become a full-time actor. It was a big moment and one that he appreciated and respected, having learned from the false dawn of *Band of Brothers* that success and stardom cannot be expected, even at the most promising of times.

In the summer of 2004 he flew out to Canada to star in a TV movie called *A Bear Named Winnie*. This charming tale centred on the origin of the Winnie the Pooh stories written by AA Milne and starred Stephen Fry as a zookeeper and David Suchet as an army general. Michael thoroughly enjoyed filming because he got to work with three adorable black bear cubs.

In the film he played Lt. Harry Colebourn of the Canadian Army Veterinary Corps who, on a whim, bought a bear cub from a hunter in Ontario in 1914. The English-born Colebourn named her Winnie, after his adopted hometown of Winnipeg. Later, the bear accompanied him to England where he was posted to a militia cavalry regiment called The Fort Garry Horse. Here Winnie became an unofficial mascot of the regiment, with whom Colebourn worked as a veterinarian. When he was sent to France in 1914, he donated the bear to London Zoo. It was here that she became a big favourite with a young boy named Christopher Robin, who liked to visit the zoo with his father, Alan Alexander Milne. Christopher Robin even changed the name of his teddy bear, Edward Bear, to Winnie, and they became inseparable. AA Milne was charmed by the way his son talked and played with the bear and this inspired him to write his first Winnie the Pooh book in 1926. After the war, Colebourn planned to take Winnie back to Canada but when he saw how children were so enchanted by her, he changed his mind and she lived at London Zoo for 20 years.

Back home in Killarney, Josef and Adele were delighted that their son was making a go of his career and was now able to do it full time. He went back to visit them frequently and always over Christmas and the New Year if he wasn't working.

Following the charm of *A Bear Named Winnie*, his next role could hardly have been in sharper contrast, as a psychotic serial killer with a foot fetish! It was in a BBC TV Sherlock Holmes drama in which Rupert Everett took on the role of the legendary sleuth in *Sherlock Holmes and the Case of the Silk Stocking*, with Ian Hart as Dr Watson. The film, shown on Boxing Day 2004, was not written by Holmes's creator, Conan Doyle, but was an original screenplay by scriptwriter Allan Cubitt.

The rather odd story had a sinister-looking Michael playing a character with a foot fetish who gets his kicks by strangling aristocratic young women with one of their own stockings and sticking the other one down their throat. Holmes investigates after the body of a 17-year-old girl fished out of the River Thames is found to be Lady Alice, daughter of the Duke and Duchess of Marlborough. When a previous victim of the same killer is identified as a ladies maid, Sarah O'Brien, Holmes suspects Charles Allen, the footman for the Duke and Duchess who formerly worked for the same aristocratic family as Sarah. Meanwhile, the daughter of Lord and Lady Massingham, Lady Georgina, is found dead, hanging from a lamppost in London with a stocking around her neck and another in her mouth.

Another young girl is attacked but survives to tell the tale and positively identifies Allen as her attacker when Holmes brings him in for questioning. This marks Michael's first appearance in the film after almost an hour as the surly footman with a sinister sneer. To Holmes's frustration, Allen's fingerprints do not match those found on a bottle of brandy that the killer used to drug his victim with a sleeping draft. What's more, Allen has a cast-iron alibi. On the day of the two most recent murders he attended the Duchess at two formal occasions where he was seen by hundreds of people. Holmes is convinced Allen is the killer, but how is he getting away with it? He later realises that the only possible solution is that Allen has an identical twin brother who is aiding him in his dastardly deeds.

So, despite his late entrance in the drama, Michael later gets double the exposure when Holmes and Watson fight the Allen twins, with Michael playing the dual roles. In playing the fetish fiend, Michael had some creepy scenes, kissing and caressing young women's feet. Several critics thought the acting and photography was fine but that the plot fizzled out rather lamely. 'Even if the surprise ending was something of a cop-out, it still managed to grip; and it was beautifully shot,' said the *Sunday Times*.

'On the whole it worked extremely well. The production was stylish, dark and atmospheric with a classic London pea-souper serving as a Dickensian metaphor for the moral murk beyond the brightly lit Edwardian interiors,' commented *The Times*, while the *Observer* considered it to be 'a real treat'.

The *Daily Express* was less impressed. 'Unfortunately, the story – a brand new one, written by Allan Cubitt, about a deranged serial killer who abducted society debutantes – was full of ridiculous anachronisms and owed more to *The Silence Of The Lambs* than Sir Arthur Conan Doyle,' it said.

A pattern was forming in which Michael either played loveable, charming characters or nasty, evil ones. Casting directors seemed to think that his ability to appear brooding could be seen as either heroic or malicious and his distinctive wide grin as either sweet or sinister. It enabled him to play a variety of roles and the work came rolling in.

The popular ITV1 drama series *William and Mary* co-starred Martin Clunes and Julie Graham in the title roles as an undertaker and a midwife who become romantically involved. It was a warm-hearted drama that appealed to a Sunday-night TV audience. In the third episode of the third series Michael played a handsome Latvian chef named Lukasz, whose partner Rosie (Clara Salaman) is pregnant with his baby. With the birth imminent, Mary and her fellow midwife and best friend Doris (Claire Hackett) visit and Doris, who fancies Lukasz, is pleased to see him in a tight white vest. At first, Lukasz helps Rosie through her contractions by holding her hand but then he makes an excuse to go in the kitchen. Mary has a quiet word with him, persuading him to join Rosie in the home-birthing pool, and an excited Doris changes her seat to get a better view as he walks in and strips to his underpants! But after the baby is successfully delivered, he makes a play for Mary before walking out on Rosie.

Michael was to take on a far more devilish role in Sky One's supernatural series *Hex*, which was generally regarded as Britain's answer to the hugely successful US teen show, *Buffy The Vampire Slayer*. Filmed to the same high-quality standards, it was shot on location at the magnificent Englefield House in Berkshire, which doubled as the fictitious English school, Medenham Hall, set on the site of an 18th-century scandal when the Medenham Witches were tried and executed.

When the rather shy Cassie (Christina Cole) enrols at the school, her latent telekinetic and clairvoyant abilities are awakened whenever she touches an antique vase that had been used in voodoo rituals by the Medenham witches. Her roommate, Thelma (Jemima Rooper), who has a crush on her, discovers that Cassie is a descendent of the witches. Unfortunately for Cassie, she attracts the attention of Azazeal, played by Michael with slicked-backed hair and a quiet, moody menace. He is the leader of fallen angels who call themselves Nephilim and who were kicked out of heaven for sleeping with mortal women. Azazeal declares his love for Cassie but secretly just wants a child by her so that it will be one more Nephilim in the mortal world.

Despite her misgivings, Cassie finds herself falling for the charismatic and handsome Azazeal and falls increasingly under his power, even after he kills Thelma who is thereafter seen as a ghost. As his hold over Cassie strengthens, she gives in to him and ultimately conceives his child. But after Thelma tells Cassie what the birth of the baby will mean, she tries to abort it. Cassie thinks she has successfully done so but the doctor who carried it out was influenced by Azazeal, and the baby, without her knowing, has been born and is being cared for by Azazeal – a son he names Malachi.

A second series followed in which a sexy new student, Ella, joins the school and seems to know about Cassie and

Azazeal. Her leather corsets are an instant hit with the boys, causing jealousy among the girls, but she is a lot older than she looks. In fact she's a 445-year-old witch who had been hunting Azazeal for centuries to prevent him from having a son by a mortal witch. But this time she's arrived too late and the only answer is to kill Malachi. Later in the series Cassie dies after she and Ella kidnap Malachi but are confronted by Azazeal. The focus is then on Ella's battle with her nemesis.

At his most threatening and frightening moment, Azazeal transforms into the demon creature that lurks beneath his handsome, mortal visage. This required Michael to spend six hours wearing a wetsuit while they made a latex mould of his body to turn him into the demon, and he sat patiently while make-up and prosthetics were applied to his face and body. Fortunately all the demon scenes in the series were shot in one day, so he didn't have to keep enduring it.

Laura Pyper, who played Ella, is a fellow Irish actress from Magherafelt in Co. Derry and she saw instantly how easy it was to come under Michael's spell! 'Michael's a bit of a heart-throb,' she told the Irish newspaper the *Sunday Life*. 'He has this amazing quality where you turn a camera on him and he's just to die for – full of charisma and very, very charming.'

For his part, Michael enjoyed the frequent snogging scenes with his pretty, blonde-haired co-star Christina Cole. 'The more times I got to do that the better,' he told the *Sunday Mirror*. 'Just, you know, it makes a happier environment to come to work to and you know that, if you can have a laugh while you're doing creative stuff and you're getting the work done as well, that's great.'

The show was generally well received with the *Sunday Times* saying, 'The punchy script and natty lesbian sidekick make this a promising start.' The *Sunday People* said, 'This stylish supernatural drama is a grown-up thrilling chiller. Forget *Buffy*, *Bewitched* and *Charmed* – this is not for those of us of a nervous disposition.' But the *Observer* was less than impressed: 'It would be easy to describe this rather predictable series as a British *Buffy the Vampire Slayer*, which would appeal to many, but this viewer was left with the feeling of having seen it all before.'

The month after *Hex* started showing on Sky One and began building up an impressive fan base, Michael began filming on the popular BBC1 cop drama *Murphy's Law*, which starred James Nesbitt in the title role of undercover cop, DS Tommy Murphy. The third series focussed on one story which began with Murphy posing as a gun dealer who becomes deeper involved in crime when a buyer named Caz Miller, played by Michael, mentions that the gun is to be used for a hit. Murphy then goes undercover as a hitman and discovers that Miller works for well-known gangster Dave Callard (Mark Womack), who has been using his ill-gotten gains for legitimate enterprises and wants to kill an employee, Richard Holloway, who is supposedly sleeping with his wife.

The *Observer* called the final episode, in which Callard, Miller and Murphy go into hiding, 'a grand finale to this ambitious series, which has successfully raised the bar for British detective drama'.

Michael drew on his German heritage once more to play a German POW in a BBC Four drama called *Hidden Lives*, based on the best-selling book by Simon Garfield. Beginning in the 1930s, more than 1,000 'ordinary' people volunteered to chronicle their daily lives. These diaries were compiled for the Mass Observation Project, described as 'an anthropology of ourselves'. In his book, *Our Hidden Lives*, Simon Garfield selected five of the most interesting diarists and focused on the post-war years from 1945 to 1948, providing a remarkable picture of how people coped in Britain during this period when the austerity seemed to drag on and on.

In the TV adaptation, Michael's character has a sexual relationship with an older man, a snobbish gay antiques dealer who lives in Edinburgh, played by Ian McDiarmid. This required the actors to be half naked in bed together. It was an awkward scene for both of them but Michael didn't shy away from such things. Stripping naked for his first appearance on TV had lessened his inhibitions!

By now, Michael was gaining a reputation as a versatile actor, not afraid to take on challenging roles, playing characters that were not necessarily likeable and, in some cases, distinctly unpleasant – psychotic murderers, callous boyfriends, violent criminals and demonic 'angels' among them.

In an episode of *Agatha Christie's Poirot*, called *After the Funeral*, he played an upper-class Englishman named George Abernethie who is believed to be the sole beneficiary in his uncle Richard's will. But after Richard's death, the family seem surprised to hear that he had disinherited his favourite nephew and shared his wealth among the others. The two had supposedly argued recently but the family lawyer, George Entwhistle, suspects the new may be a forgery and he has reason to be even more suspicious when Richard's eccentric sister Cora remarks at the funeral, 'It's been hushed up very nicely ... but he was murdered, wasn't he?'

Richard, 68 and a widower, had lost his only child, Mortimer, to polio six months earlier. Mortimer, who was about to marry, died with no issue and so Richard needed to revise his will. He was the eldest of a family of seven, of which only he, a reclusive brother Timothy and a sister Cora, the youngest, are still alive. As well as his nephew, George, Richard had two nieces, Susan and Rosamund – the children of siblings who have already died. His decision was to split his wealth into six portions, for his five blood relations and a sixth for Helen, the widow of a beloved brother killed in the recent war.

The day after the funeral Cora is beaten to death in her sleep and Entwhistle calls on his old friend Poirot (David Suchet) to investigate. Poirot questions the family members at Richard's magnificent estate, Enderby, for which Rotherfield Park in Hampshire was used. The motive for Cora's murder is unclear. There was no theft. But her timid maid, Miss Gilchrist, tells how she overheard Richard telling Cora that he suspected he was being poisoned. Has she been murdered to stop her from speaking out? Poirot warns Entwhistle that Miss Gilchrist may herself be a target for the murderer.

Cora had been a keen artist and collector of paintings from local sales. The day after her funeral, an art critic friend of hers arrives to evaluate her most recent acquisitions. His visit had been planned before her death, but he finds nothing of value. That evening, Miss Gilchrist is nearly killed by arsenic poison in a slice of wedding cake apparently sent to her through the post.

In typical Agatha Christie fashion, there are plenty of red herrings. None of the family is above suspicion as they were all alone on the day of Cora's murder with no firm alibis. Susan, who inherits her Aunt Cora's property, is married to dispensing chemist Gregory, who had been responsible for deliberately administering a non-lethal overdose to an awkward customer. The other niece, Rosamund, is hiding a secret, which turns out to be her husband's infidelity and her own pregnancy. The unpleasant Timothy Abernethie might have been able to commit the murder of Cora, as might his wife, Maude and so, too, could the seemingly genteel Helen. Or perhaps George himself might have killed his uncle in anger after their argument.

But then something occurs to Helen and she telephones

Entwhistle with the news that she has realised what struck her as odd on the day of the funeral. But before she can say what it is she is hit on the head. While Helen is away recovering, Poirot – ever the one for a sense of theatre – gathers everyone to Enderby Hall for the denouement. It's gasps and dropped jaws all round as he reveals that it wasn't Cora at Richard's funeral but Miss Gilchrist in disguise. She had put a sedative in Cora's tea and left her at home while she attended the funeral and reading of the will. None of the family had seen Cora for over 20 years so fooling them wasn't too difficult. She wished to plant the idea that Richard's death had been murder so that, when Cora herself was murdered, it would seem that the same attacker was responsible.

Miss Gilchrist had copied Cora's mannerisms, in particular a characteristic turn of her head. But Helen had realised that 'Cora' had turned her head to the left, not the right. Miss Gilchrist had made the mistake of practising in a mirror without taking on board that the reflection was a reverse of reality. She had deliberately poisoned herself with the arsenic-laced wedding cake to avoid suspicion.

It transpires that Miss Gilchrist was sure that one of the paintings Cora had recently bought was by Vermeer. Aware that her art-critic friend was bound to recognise it when he visited the following day, Miss Gilchrist hastily hatched a plot and covered the Vermeer with a painting she had done herself. But she was unable to cover up the fresh scent of the paint. Once accused, Miss Gilchrist breaks down and admits that she murdered Cora because she hated her and desperately wanted enough money to be able to rebuild her beloved teashop, which she had had to close during the war because of food shortages. There is no evidence of foul play regarding Richard Abernethie's death.

Michael was utterly convincing, playing the rude, self-centred, hard drinking and gambling George Abernethie with a posh English accent.

The long-running TV series *Trial & Retribution*, created by Lynda La Plante, was a gritty and superior procedural cop drama that, in each story, showed the crime, the investigation and the trial. It starred David Hayman as DCS Mike Walker and later, Victoria Smurfit as DCI Roisin Connor. In 2006 Michael filmed the two-part story, *Sins of the Father*, which was shown on ITV1 in January of the following year.

The story revolved around pretty teenager Emily Harrogate (played by Carey Mulligan), the daughter of a seemingly happily married middle-class family. When she is found dead at the bottom of the cellar stairs by her parents John and Deirdre, the marks on her neck and the force with which she fell suggest she was attacked. When Connor and DS Satchell investigate, they discover that this outwardly stable family is falling apart. It emerges that John is having an affair with a work colleague and that his troubled teenage son, James, cannot provide an alibi for his whereabouts on the night of Emily's death. A breakthrough in the case comes when an eyewitness leads the cops to a teenage neighbour, Michael Summerby (Andrew Lee Potts), who was Emily's secret boyfriend. His flimsy alibi makes him the number-one suspect and he is eventually charged with her murder.

Michael played the lad's defence barrister, Douglas Nesbitt. He has little to work with, since Summerby cannot provide an alibi. Then, while in court, Summerby all but confesses to being responsible for her death, stating that he 'was to blame'. He confesses that he was in her parents' house at the time of her death and that she was hysterically backing away from him before falling down the cellar stairs. The jury have little trouble in pronouncing him guilty but it's a miscarriage of justice. John and his son James are hiding a secret and John is quite prepared to destroy the life of an innocent man.

For a change, Michael was able to play the barrister as an Irishman and his calm and methodical courtroom demeanour contrasted well with the excitable and emotional performance by an impressive Andrew Lee Potts.

Towards the end of 2005 Michael started a gruelling 10 weeks of physical training. It wasn't just a keep-fit routine; rather it was the prelude to a movie that was to bring him to the consciousness of America.

CHAPTER FIVE

HOLLYWOOD VIA ANCIENT GREECE

For a shy man, the idea of appearing larger than life on cinema screens in bikini-style leather trunks and little else may have sounded rather daunting but Michael took it in his stride. After all, he had appeared butt naked in a TV commercial!

The stylised sand-and-sandals movie *300* took a very modern approach to dramatising an ancient battle. It was a story that resonated with Michael because he had been taught it at primary school back in Killarney – how in 480 BC King Leonidas mustered 300 super-fit Spartans to fight a massive Persian army marching towards Greece. The Spartans headed towards a narrow pass at Thermopylae to give themselves a fighting chance and a fierce battle took place before they were eventually overwhelmed by the Persians.

Director Zak Snyder, who had directed the 2004 zombie flick *Dawn of the Dead*, wanted to create a visually strong movie based on the graphic novel by Frank Miller, so that the scenes in the ancient tale resembled high-quality comic-book art. There would be much use of CGI and other high-tech special effects but the main cast of Spartans would not be allowed to rely on such wizardry to get into shape. So in September 2005, after Michael had been cast as the impassioned young warrior Stelios, he and five other wannabe Spartans were sent to boot camp for 10 weeks of intensive training to get their bodies in shape.

For four hours a day, five days a week, they ran, lifted weights and used all manner of gym equipment, all of which gave new meaning to the hoary old actor's phrase of 'suffering for my art'. 'We knew we were going to have to wear leather Speedos and very little else in the film,' said Michael. 'They let us eat whatever we wanted but the workouts were brutal.'

But the punishing regime produced impressive results so that, by the time they started filming in November, they were in better shape than they had ever been. Their costumes consisted of tight and skimpy leather pants, red cloaks and sandals, which caused a fair amount of sniggering and mickey-taking among the mainly British cast, which included Gerard Butler as Leonidas, Lean

Heady as his queen, Gorgo, Vincent Regan as Captain and Dominic West as the manipulative politician, Theron.

The movie was visually stunning, with the characters looking like drawings come to life against a dramatic backdrop of cliff tops, towering buildings and storm-lashed seas, with much use of high and low perspective. Red robes and a liberal amount of blood added slashes of vivid colour to grey or blue backgrounds. Together with dramatic and artistic posturing, it suggested comic-book art as well as the finest Biblical paintings from the old masters.

The story was a blood-fest from start to finish, with heads being cut off and flying through the air, soldiers charging on horses with swords aloft, bows and arrows and spears. But the cast saw little of this, as most of it was added by computer at a later stage. 'The actors, very often working up to sixteen hours a day, were surrounded by a giant blank green screen and nothing else,' explained Michael. 'My training for the theatre was very useful. When you are working live in the theatre you may be looking out over an audience but you are imagining another environment.

'In our mind's eye we would project onto the screen the invading hordes of Persian soldiers or a vast landscape or extreme climate conditions – whatever was required – and take on the physicality of that. In those conditions the actors are thrown back onto the relationships and dynamics between themselves, which is exactly how it is in the theatre.'

But the rather camp atmosphere of muscular men in bulging leather pants gave rise to much mirth between takes, with some of the jokes being borrowed from the Monty Python team's classic Biblical comedy, *Life of Brian*. As Michael told *The Times*, 'There were a lot of *Life of Brian* gags, and certainly when Dominic West walked on in his full costume, someone did say, "He wanks as high as any man in Wome!" But that just helps to get it out of your system, so there's none of it left in the film itself.'

Michael considered Zack Snyder to be an inspirational director and he welcomed Gerard Butler's supportive comments during filming. 'We had scenes together and he'd be like, "Nice work, you'll do well,"' he recalled. 'Things that are nice to hear when you're lower down on the rung.'

300 was also Michael's first Hollywood film and he was impressed by the size of his trailer. 'I thought to myself, "Why did I bother getting a flat? I could have just lived in this!"'

On its release *300* was a huge box-office success but film critics, although agreeing on its visual merit, were generally not so enthusiastic about the storytelling. The *Irish Times* called it 'a stylised, violent and heady cinematic experience'. *The Times* said, 'It's exhilarating stuff, and Snyder gets the most out of every cent of what was reportedly a comparatively low budget. Still, you start to tire of all the macho posturing and male bonding.' To the *Observer* it was 'a ridiculous rendering of the ancient world' and the influential Roger Ebert in the *Chicago Sun-Times* said, '*300* has one-dimensional caricatures who talk like professional wrestlers plugging their next feud.'

The critic from the *Sunday Telegraph* appeared to waver between like and dislike – 'This film is historically one-dimensional, ethically distasteful and frequently ludicrous. It is also, however, hardly ever boring' – but the *Daily Mail* was as sure-footed as a sandal-clad Spartan in its scathing review. 'Messrs Miller and Snyder have joined forces to make the most preposterous picture of 2007,' it said. 'It's hilariously humourless, violently homophobic yet weirdly camp – a unique, if hardly praiseworthy, combination.'

Despite the critics' opinions, *300* made a huge impact: it was tremendously successful and brought Michael to the attention of America. After his premature attempt to crack America following *Band of Brothers*, Michael had waited to have another go and now the time was right. 'After *300*, I thought, "All right, I'm in a good position now to come back and get an agent."' But his next move was a step back to his early days of acting.

Since leaving drama school Michael's acting work had been almost exclusively for television, so he welcomed the chance to tread the boards at the Edinburgh Festival Fringe in 2006. There he appeared in a play by the journalist Mary Kenny called *Allegiance*, based on a meeting in London in 1921 between Winston Churchill – at that time colonial secretary in David Lloyd George's government – and Michael Collins to discuss an Anglo-Irish peace treaty and a measure of independence for Ireland.

In this fictitious account of their meeting, the two men – with widely different upbringings, political beliefs and ambitions – start off wary of each other and then enjoy the cut and thrust of conversation on subjects such as imperialism and resistance. Later they discover an empathy with each other and there is a touching moment when Churchill – played by Mel Smith – cries at the memory of his deceased youngest daughter and Collins instinctively puts a consoling hand on his opponent's shoulder.

Michael was both excited and amused to be playing Collins, aware of his family's belief that they are descended from the legendary Irish revolutionary. For her part, author Kenny, a columnist with the *Irish Independent*, said she was thrilled that such a good-looking man as Michael Fassbender was to play Collins. She told the newspaper, 'Michael Collins was a devastatingly handsome man – all the newspapers at the time mentioned his stunning appearance. Michael Fassbender is perfect casting to Mel Smith's wonderful portrayal of a thoughtful, sometimes brooding Winston.'

The play ran for a week at Edinburgh's Assembly Rooms to generally good, although varied, reviews. The *Sunday Times* commented, 'Smith handles adequately enough an almost impossible part.' But it was far less complimentary about Michael's portrayal: 'As Collins, Fassbender is too oikish by far. Collins's myth derives, in part at least, from his hard-edged charisma and Fassbender's performance has none of it. The shortcomings of Fassbender, however, are as nothing compared with the stasis of the production and the theatrical illiteracy of Kenny's script. Collins and Churchill sound as if they have swallowed encyclopaedias.'

The *Independent*, by contrast, was impressed by both men. 'With his jowl spilling over his collar, his neck stiffening and his fingers wagging, Smith has slipped most convincingly into Churchill's shoes. He smacks his lips, sometimes swallows his words and punctuates sentences with a gravelly grunt. Fassbender endows Collins with a magnetism and quiet intelligence. An absorbing entertainment.'

The *Guardian* added, 'As is so often the case with drama in Edinburgh, the play feels more like a snippet than a fully-fledged play, and it comes from that old-school drama where people talk endlessly at each other. But the piece mostly transcends these limitations, and Fassbender and Smith are excellent.'

Michael's next move was back to the big screen. French director François Ozon has made a name for himself with such movies as *8 Women*, *Swimming Pool*, *5x2* and *Water Drops on Burning Rocks*. But it was to Edwardian London that he turned to make his first English-language movie, *Angel (The Real Life of Angel Deverell)*. Based on the 1957 book by English novelist Elizabeth Taylor, it was inspired by Marie Corelli, a contemporary of Oscar Wilde and Queen Victoria's favourite writer.

The film follows the rise and fall of an ambitious romantic novelist, Angelica 'Angel' Deverell, at the turn of the 20th century. The 15-year-old Angel dreams of becoming a writer and leaving her life above her mother's grocery shop behind. The magnificent Paradise House nearby symbolises for her the finest things she wants in life. Although her writing might not be very good, it attracts the attention of a London publisher (Sam Neill) and her subsequent books earn her a fortune. Later she comes into contact with two siblings – struggling artist Esmé, who becomes infatuated with Angel, and his sister Nora.

Romola Garai – who had played the teenage Briony Tallis in *Atonement* and the title role in the TV adaptation of Jane Austen's *Emma* – was cast as Angelica. Michael was so keen to work with Ozon that he endured five auditions before he was finally given the role of her love interest and later husband, the broody and penniless artist, Esmé. 'I really wanted to work with him because he is so open to ideas,' Michael said later, but he had found the preliminaries nerve-racking. 'I had no idea if he'd pick me. I really wanted to work with him but I was nervous. Five auditions, for God's sake!'

The magnificent, Gothic-style Tyntesfield House (near

Bristol) – with its spiralling turrets, terraced lawns, interior balconies, oak-panelled walls and estate – was used for Paradise House, which Angelica buys.

Ozon revealed that a Hollywood studio had been interested in making the film with him but he had refused after they insisted that he work with an American screenwriter for a year and come up with a happy ending. 'If I did that, they promised they'd get me an American star!' he scoffed. 'I preferred doing the film my way, with lesser-known actors and a smaller budget. I worked with a wonderful English casting director who introduced me to the current crop of young British actors. I did careful screen tests and chose actors who were enthusiastic and available, and who hadn't yet gotten their big break in England.'

He chose Romala Garai because he felt she really understood the role and wasn't afraid of the more grotesque aspects of Angel's character. Plus she brought charm and naivety to the part. He chose Michael to play Esmé because he sensed a strong chemistry between the two actors. 'The young painter needed to be real, carnal, charismatic, insolent. Michael Fassbender has those qualities; he's a mix of irony and brute force. He's Irish; he has a different accent and a different manner than the English. He's more quirky and raw.'

Ozon was impressed by his experience of working with English actors and thought they added something new to the process. 'They brought depth and complexity to the scenes, along with a level of acting that I have rarely seen,' he said. 'They prepared their roles in advance, using my indications and our conversations to really get inside their characters and bring them to life. Whereas French actors tend to work on a day-by-day basis, English actors are more like distance runners.'

For the role Michael actually had to paint – a skill, along with a knowledge of the subject of art, which he freely admits that he does not possess. 'I've got two left hands,' he said. 'I'm intimidated by a blank canvas. For me, art is about how you see the world around you and how you express it.' But there was an artist on set to advise him and they spent a lot of time ensuring that he looked professional in his approach to the canvas. He even had to be taught how to hold a paintbrush correctly.

Michael was surprised to find that Ozon actually operated the camera as well as directing. He told Michael that he was unable to visualise what he was doing if he's not looking through a lens. The pair discussed whether Esmé and Angel genuinely loved each other or if their relationship was just a move to benefit him financially. They decided that he never really loved Angel but had convinced himself that he did. 'Esmé is the black sheep of the family,' Michael explained. 'He lives to enjoy his life on a sensual level with women, gambling and drink, but he's frustrated and insecure. He's a contradiction. He tries to appear blasé but he actually cares very deeply about his work, which everyone else thinks is rubbish.

'She's such a strong personality and so different, even nerdy, and all those things appeal to him,' he said. 'She awakens something in him that other women never have when it comes to his work. She trusts him and lets him into her world, which knocks him off balance, unsettles him and therefore interests him.'

But Angel is also manipulative, unpleasant and egotistical. This initially worried Michael because he felt she needed some redeeming qualities. 'When I first read the script, I longed for her to do something nice,' he said. 'It was something that concerned me right up till we started filming but, once I saw the way François filmed it and Romola played her, I realised that you couldn't help admiring Angel. Her belief in herself and determination to do what she wants to do in a world dominated by men is quite something. If you walk away from the film unmoved, with no admiration or pity for her, you've missed the main idea of the film.

'I think you have to feel sorry for her. Here is this creature constructing her life as she does her books: she decides what love should be, what her life should be, how important her status in society is, but I don't think she gets any genuine pleasure or nourishment out of any of it. I mean, look at the sex! She does it because she thinks that is what is required, rather than from any real desire.'

Following a formal press conference for *Angel* in Rome, Michael was interviewed by the pretty Italian actress Marina Limosani for TV. At least, she was trying to interview Michael but it was a long-winded procedure because he does not speak Italian and she only understood a little English, so a middle-aged Italian man interpreted her questions to Michael and then interpreted his replies in Italian straight to camera. It would have been difficult for anyone to engage properly with the questions under such circumstances: there are long, awkward pauses in the footage and Michael looks a little bemused. But it is also clear that he has other things on his mind – he flirts outrageously with a coquettish Marina.

As she introduces him to the viewers he interrupts her with a question of his own: 'What's your boyfriend's name?' She grins and blushes while he smiles and laughs. The sexual tension between them is evident as he continues to glance at her while the straight-faced interpreter talks to camera. She flicks her hair back and bites her bottom lip, looking a little embarrassed. With the interpreter carrying on oblivious to what is going on behind him, Michael jokingly tries to sneak a look at the questions on her sheet of paper. She pulls it away and they both grin and he whispers, 'I can't read Italian.'

Later, a high-spirited Michael puts his arm around the interpreter and playfully remarks, 'I love this guy.' At the end of the interview he puts his arms around them both and encourages them to join him as he launches into a few lines from Mozart's *The Marriage of Figaro*, singing the aria *Se vuol ballare*, in which Figaro vows his revenge on the Count who is plotting to sleep with his fiancé, Susanna.

The Italian pair are flummoxed and do not know the words but Michael carries on regardless.

The film, however, was critically panned. 'A formulaic period film,' said the *Daily Mirror*. 'This really is a failure – an honourable failure, arguably, but a failure, and a pretty complete one at that,' said the *Guardian*. For its part the *Express* considered the film a missed opportunity: 'A major disappointment, feeling creaky and clumsy in a way you wouldn't expect from the director of *Under the Sand* and *8 Women*.' The *Observer* was one of the few to be upbeat, calling it a 'fascinating film curio'.

In the same year Michael had a small role in a Channel 4 TV comedy drama that was as far removed from the glamour of *Angel* as you can imagine. Written by *Trainspotting* author Irvine Welsh, *Wedding Belles* was an earthy and ribald piece set in the working-class community of Leith, Edinburgh, which focused on the lives and loves of four women who have been lifelong friends.

As Amanda (Michelle Gomez), a hairdresser on probation for GBH, prepares to marry the man of her dreams – airline pilot Joshua – her pals take stock of their own lives, which have failed to live up to their dreams. Ex-fashion model Rhona (Shauna Macdonald) is still mourning the death of her fiancé and falling into drug dependency. Kelly (Shirley Henderson) is battling her demons and managing to upset all those around her and Shaz (Kathleen McDermott) works in an old people's home, selling black-market Viagra to the residents.

In his brief appearance as a character called Barney Ross, a former love of Amanda's and recently released from prison for armed robbery, Michael had a memorable dance scene. People give way to him when, full of swagger, he struts onto a club dance floor wearing a black suit with red shoes and tie. His stylistic, high-kicking movements are reminiscent of John Travolta in *Saturday Night Fever*.

With its scenes of Viagra-fuelled lust in an old people's home, drug taking and sex with a Catholic priest, *Wedding Belles* chimed with some while others thought it a clanger. The critics too were divided. The *Guardian* described is as a 'dire comedy drama' while the *Sunday Times* lambasted Welsh for being an author who has 'mined the same thin vein of inspiration for far too long and now comes up with more dross than ore'. But the *Observer* enjoyed the pace and quality of the production, commenting, 'What stopped *Wedding Belles* looking like parody was not only the acting but the directing and the photography and the editing and the music and the sheer hard-nosed, breathlessly bloody-minded energy of it all. If you like your drama dark and down and dirty, you'd be pushed to find a better example.' And to the *Daily Telegraph* it was 'a fabulously noirish piece of entertainment'.

In the summer of 2006 Michael also had a cameo role in Woody Allen's *Cassandra's Dream*. The film, set in

London, starred Colin Farrell and Ewan McGregor as brothers Terry and Ian, who are hard up for cash. When gambler Terry (Farrell) has a big win at the greyhound track, he splashes out on a sailing boat that he names *Cassandra's Dream*, after the dog that won the race. They enjoy taking the boat out onto the water but the name turns out to be a bad omen: they are blissfully unaware that *Cassandra's Dream* refers to the ancient Greek seer whose accurate prophecies of doom went unheeded by those around her.

Terry's good luck doesn't last long and he ends up owing a lot of money to a violent loan shark who warns him to pay up or suffer the consequences. Around this time, the brothers' successful businessman uncle Howard (Tom Wilkinson) arrives in town, looking for a favour from his nephews. He admits that he is about to go to jail because of accusations from his business partner, who plans to testify against him. There's only one way to silence him. After initial reluctance, the two brothers agree to murder him in exchange for Howard paying their financial debts.

Although he was only in the film for a brief period, Michael jumped at the chance to work with the acclaimed director and thoroughly enjoyed the way in which he operated. 'Working with Woody Allen was a learning experience,' he told the *Irish Times*. 'He gives a lot of space to the actors to find their own way into a character or through a scene. I was also impressed by the way Allen finished each working day by 4pm, which is unusual in film, so that he could spend time with his family. And you have to admire his ability to raise funding for projects that really aren't mainstream.'

But if Michael was impressed by Allen, it was hard to find others who were, once the movie was released. 'A clumsy, clichéd morality play that may actually represent the lowest point of Allen's recently chequered career,' said *Empire* magazine. 'This feels like it was knocked together by complete amateurs,' said the *Guardian*. To the *Daily Telegraph* it was a 'lead-footed fiasco' and the *Independent* was equally as blunt: 'Quite stupefyingly terrible.'

By this time Michael had begun a relationship with Australian singer Maiko Spencer and the pair had started living together in a London flat. She is the stepdaughter of the actor Sam Neill, who had married her Japanese mother, make-up artist Noriko Watanabe. Maiko had led a cosmopolitan life, growing up in Sydney and then moving to New York before settling in London.

The year 2007 was to be a turning point in Michael's fortunes in a big way. After a visit back to Fossa in April to see his parents and celebrate his 30th birthday with friends and family, he flew to Romania to start shooting the Joel Schumacher horror movie *Town Creek*, later renamed *Blood Creek*. Schumacher, who had helmed the likes of *St Elmo's Fire*, *Batman Forever* and *Batman and Robin*, was one of Michael's favourite directors, so he was excited to be working with him.

The beginning of this tale of terror takes place in 1936, as the Wollners – a poverty-stricken German-American family living in Town Creek, West Virginia – are contacted by the Nazi Third Reich with a lucrative offer to host a visiting scholar, Professor Richard Wirth, played by Michael. But Wirth – all slicked-back hair, suit and tie – is not an ideal dinner companion. On his first night in the house he points out that Germany will soon rule the world. He is, in fact, on a secret mission for the Nazi regime to recover ancient Viking artefacts that can bestow immortality. Outside in the barn, which the family have built on a Viking stone, he touches the stone and gains the power to bring back to life their daughter's dead bird. Oblivious to the occult experiments being conducted around them by Wirth, the Wollners take him in – a decision that will haunt their family and their town for decades.

The story then jumps forward to 2007 when Victor Marshall (Dominic Purcell) vanishes into thin air while camping near Town Creek. Determined to discover the true fate of his missing brother, Evan Marshall (Henry Cavill) searches for answers. But just when it appears that none are to be found, Victor reappears, mysteriously saying that he had been abducted and tortured for two years. The brothers pack guns and return to Town Creek determined on revenge but they encounter a super-powerful Wirth who is able to command the dead to do his bidding.

The movie had a limited release before going to DVD but it gained a cult following. 'Blood Creek is dumb, gory, post-pub fun,' said Total Film magazine. The sci-fi and horror magazines and websites thought it enjoyable in the main. 'This is a whole new side of Joel Schumacher and I like it,' said horrornews.net. 'Despite its flaws, Blood Creek is dark, intriguing, energetic and at times brutal.' But Starburst magazine thought that Michael was wasting his time. 'Michael Fassbender seems like he is slumming it here and gets the best from the scenes he is in but really feels wasted when we know he is capable of so much more.'

But Michael was enjoying the variety of his roles and the directors and actors he was working with. All the time he was learning his craft, taking it very seriously and pleased that he was getting so much work. From the end of July to September 2007 he began shooting another scary movie called Eden Lake.

In this he played middle-class Steve who drives to the countryside with his girlfriend Jenny (Kelly Reilly) for a romantic day by the lakeside, where he plans to propose to her. But while lounging by the lake their peace is disturbed by the noise of five hoodie teenagers with blaring music and a Rottweiler. In what The Times called 'one of the most terrifying movie moments of 2008', Steve approaches to ask them to turn the music down. It's a fateful moment that will lead to him getting beaten up, tied and stabbed as one of the teenagers records it on a mobile phone. The terrified couple end up running for their lives after their romantic day has turned into horror.

It was a grim, tense but engrossing movie about the violence of youth and the clash of different cultures in a remote setting and echoed such movies as *Deliverance*, *Straw Dogs* and *Clockwork Orange*. Written and directed by James Watkins, it was filmed in Buckinghamshire at Frensham Ponds, Black Park and Burnham Beeches. 'I didn't want the couple Jenny and Steve to be the usual bland Californian Ken and Barbie horror fodder,' said Watkins. 'You know, the kind that has the audience wanting them to die. We had to care about them; we had to feel their love before we feel their pain. I deliberately kept the context on Steve and Jenny clipped and spare. I wanted them to be every young couple in the audience, making us all ask, "What would I do? Take responsibility or turn your back? Stand up or step away?"'

For Kelly, the loving relationship between Steve and Jenny was at the heart of the movie and made their grim ordeal all the more unbearable. '*Eden Lake* isn't all about the violent repercussions,' she said. 'James had exactly the right handle on the most touching moment between Jenny and Steve. Jenny doesn't know until it's too late that Steve has organised the weekend solely as a device to propose marriage. When he's fatally injured and she tries to patch him up, she comes across the Tiffany engagement ring in his pocket. It's an incredibly intimate moment, heart-breaking to play and sensitively done. Both Mike and I knew this scene had to count because it was all about what might have been, not the vicious reality of what is. Steve and Jenny's rosy future is vanishing fast and it was as solid an acting piece as I've ever had to play.'

Filming such terrifying, violent and often gruesome scenes resulted in the cast being particularly considerate to each other and having fun whenever they could, to distance themselves from the horror of the story. Thomas Turgoose, who played a gang member named Cooper, told the website *LastBroadcast*, 'Cooper's darkest moment is when he stabs Steve in the mouth. Mike was tied to a tree stump all day, barefoot, cold and uncomfortable, but not once did he complain. It clearly wasn't easy for him yet time and again he gave a great performance. I wasn't looking forward to this scene at all but Mike's hard work and good humour throughout meant it went smoothly. He always asked if I was fine because it was such a strong emotional moment for me and I really appreciated his concern.'

In the evenings the cast went out together to eat at restaurants and played games in the hotel games room. On the last day of shooting Michael took the young cast – who nicknamed him 'Fassy B' – to Thorpe Park theme park, near Slough. 'Michael Fassbender is one of the funniest guys in the world. Ultra-cool too. I never stopped laughing,' Thomas added.

Jack O'Connell, who played gang leader Brett, was impressed by how much fun Michael was off set and how focused both he and Kelly Reilly were during filming. 'Kelly and Mike were so professional and their experience really made *Eden Lake* sail along,' he remembered.

The critics loved the movie, despite its unsettling and violent nature. 'This looks to me like the best British horror film in years,' said the *Guardian*, which described Michael as 'a young and fiercely charismatic Irish actor who is suddenly and justifiably ubiquitous on our screens'. *The Times* called it 'an unexpectedly intelligent British horror film', while the *Daily Mail* said it was 'a first-rate British horror film that taps into our deepest fears'. The *People* agreed that it was 'an exciting terror flick'.

The critic from the *Sun* was one of the few who didn't like it but still praised Michael and his antagonist for their performances, 'Rising star Michael Fassbender as Steve and Jack O'Connell as Brett should be commended for maintaining the tension despite working from an implausible script.'

The 'rising star' was about to soar to new heights in his next movie, which was to be the defining moment of his career as he went from promising actor to leading man and Hollywood opened its gates.

CHAPTER SIX

A NAKED HUNGER

B ritish film artist and director Steve McQueen first became known for his short films, which were projected onto one or more walls in art galleries. His early videos were shot in black and white, were silent and he often appeared in them himself. His first major film, *Bear*, in 1993, features him and another naked man in an ambiguous encounter that could be interpreted as either threatening or erotic. His later work includes *Deadpan*, a homage to Buster Keaton in which the sides of a building fall down around him. It is repeated time and time again from many angles, while he remains motionless and expressionless. In 1999 he won the prestigious Turner Prize, beating the front-runner and more widely known Tracey Emin.

At the beginning of 2003 McQueen was approached by Jan Younghusband, head of drama and arts at Channel 4, who asked him if he would like to make a film for the their movie outlet, Film Four, which had produced such hits as *Trainspotting*, *East is East*, *My Beautiful Laundrette*, *Shallow Grave* and *The Last King of Scotland*.

McQueen, who was born and brought up in London, came up with the idea of making a film on Bobby Sands, an IRA prisoner who famously died at Maze prison, Northern Ireland, in 1981, after staging a 66 day hunger strike in protest at the British government's refusal to grant republican prisoners political status. He was just 27. Nine others went on to starve themselves to death and the protest – which included smearing his cell walls with his own excrement – gained much publicity at the time. McQueen remembered watching TV news reports about it when he was 11.

'I asked my mother and father what was going on and they told me,' he said. 'At that age, it was very difficult to understand – someone who gave up eating food in order to be heard. Twenty-seven years later, that story was still baffling me and I really needed to go and look at it visually. It was like the whole thing had never happened – the twenty-fifth anniversary of Bobby Sands' death, there was nothing in the papers, or hardly anything.'

Michael was four when Sands died and, although too young to remember it, he did recall what he described as 'the tension' of the period whenever his family travelled to

Northern Ireland to visit their relatives. Here they would routinely encounter watchtowers and armed British soldiers as they crossed the border but, as a young child, he never really understood what was happening. 'We never really discussed politics at home,' he explained. Even today he says that he is resistant to nationalism, due to 'not being quite Irish, not quite German'.

Michael got to meet McQueen and the co-writer of *Hunger*, Enda Walshe, after the casting director, Gary Davy – who had cast him in *Band of Brothers* – recommended him for the part of Bobby Sands. Michael thought Steve was different and had an honesty about him. Unfortunately for Michael, Steve took an instant dislike to him! 'I thought, "Who is this geezer?" He came with a bit of a swagger, a bit of an attitude. I thought, "I don't know if I like this guy,"' he recalled. 'He almost seemed like he couldn't be bothered.'

But Michael was later to explain his attitude as being a mix of bravado and concern over the subject matter. 'I was defensive,' Michael would later admit. 'I was an actor trying to get work, dealing with a lot of rejection and there was a stern, inquisitive side of me that was like, "What do you want to do with this story?" I've got family from the North of Ireland. And there had been films in the past that, I think, have been insulting to the people up there. So I wanted to make sure that it was being handled right.'

Michael went away thinking that his meeting with Steve had gone well but Gary Davy had to persuade Steve to see

Michael again for auditions the following day. Steve actively did not want him for the part of Sands but agreed to 'just put him in the mix'. The core of the film was to be a conversation between Sands and the parish priest halfway through, in which Sands tells him he is going on a hunger strike. For the audition, Michael read some of Sands' lines while Steve filled in as the priest. To the director's surprise, this completely changed his notion about Michael. 'He was a totally different person: extraordinarily engaged and engaging. And I thought, "This guy could play Bobby Sands."'

Delighted as he was to get the part, Michael continued to have concerns about it. 'I was worried because things are really on the mend in the North, and Belfast is a fantastic city. I didn't want to spark off anything that would, in any way, reignite that,' he explained. He was also far from confident that an audience would want to see prisoners smearing excrement on the walls or suffering. He discussed it with his parents, who were also wary of the potential dangers of the film, but they agreed it was a challenge that he should go for.

Michael also felt instinctively that he would learn something from working with McQueen, although he had never directed a feature film before. Michael was right: McQueen would bring a very artistic, stylised approached to the film, leaning on his experiments with video. There would be no dialogue for the majority of the film, relying instead on visual impact.

The experienced Irish actor, Liam Cunningham, was to play the Catholic priest, Father Dominic Moran, and the movie was to instigate a lasting friendship between the two actors. In September 2007, Michael left his London home for Belfast where filming was to take place and shooting began the following month on the crucial scene between convict and cleric. It is a long, powerful and engrossing dialogue as they spar verbally across a prison table about the rights and wrongs of a hunger strike which would likely lead to a self-imposed death – a mortal sin within the Catholic church.

Michael was to admit that he was nervous about this pivotal scene, having to learn lines that ran for 28 pages. He first met Liam Cunningham in a Belfast pub with McQueen and the two bonded by nipping outside for a cigarette. But after they came back in they felt the need for another 'calming' cigarette after the director told them that he was thinking of shooting the 23-minute long scene in one shot. 'My immediate reaction was, "Are you out of your fuckin' mind?!"' Cunningham recalled. 'I looked at Michael and just said, "I'm going to have to move in with you." He said, "Yeah, I think so."'

Michael was renting a waterfront apartment in Belfast and his co-star did indeed move into the spare room. Here they rehearsed the scene over and over, up to 15 times a day for 5 days, straight after breakfast. At 1pm a production assistant would arrive with lunch and after that they would carry on rehearsing until 6 or 7pm. Then

McQueen would turn up to check on their progress and hand them some notes, and they would resume once more before going to the pub, exhausted, for a couple of pints each. 'We knew it was essential to get it right,' said Michael. 'That conversation was the make or break. It was the beast that needed to be tamed.'

Their hard work paid off. When they filmed the scene in early October, they did four takes all the way through and the fourth take was used.

Neither actor had ever worked with someone as unconventional as McQueen before. The director used a sporting metaphor to describe the confrontation between priest and prisoner. 'I wanted to make it like a tennis match between Jimmy Connors and John McEnroe,' he said. 'Two titans battling it out in their completely different ways, yet sharing an intimacy and an understanding of each other's position.' And after one of the takes he remarked, 'It's getting a little bit like Frank Sinatra and Dean Martin. I want you to behave more like God.'

'I looked at Liam and he was like, "Ooh fuck",' said Michael. 'It sounds silly but we were maybe a third into the scene and I swear in Liam's eye and in my mind we understood what he meant.'

Seventeen minutes of the twenty-three-minute scene were filmed in a single take before the camera pulled away for a different angle and the remainder was concluded. The length of the scene also took its toll on the crew member who was holding the boom mic. 'On take three he collapsed as he had been holding that thing up there for so long,' Michael remembered.

After the scene was shot, the production was closed down for 10 weeks while Michael went on a drastic weight-loss regime in order to authentically portray a man dying from hunger. Adele pleaded with her son not to do it because she was worried that he would do himself serious harm but in the end she reluctantly accepted that he had to, for the sake of realism.

After consulting with a doctor and a nutritionist, Michael began by eating only 1,000 calories a day. 'I just knew that I had to do it,' he said. 'All the stuff we had filmed before that was pretty special and I didn't want the last part of the film to break the illusion. So I had to get super-thin.'

Michael knew he could be a disciplined person when he set his mind to it. At the age of 7 he had given up everything sweet during the 40 days of Lent and, while many of his friends had given in during St Patrick's Day, he refused to do so. But that was then. Did he still have that sort of will power – and more – aged 30?

By week two, he noticed insomnia setting in because his body was telling him to eat but he got used to dealing with that. However, he found that he was being too distracted from his strict discipline by friends who would visit his London home. 'If you are sitting down watching a film together, you can't ask people not to eat around you,' he said. So he told Maiko that he would not be seeing her for a while and rented house in Venice Beach, California, because he felt that somewhere nice and warm with clear blue skies would help. And it did. His diet consisted of blueberries and a few nuts in the morning, followed by a tin of sardines and a slice of bread for dinner.

He also found that the more he busied himself during the day, the easier it was to forget about food. And he soon learned that it was a mistake to watch television. 'I never realised how much food is on television! So I stopped watching adverts because I didn't like seeing mouth-watering burgers every fifteen minutes.'

For a few days, his sister Catherine came to stay with him. She had gained a PhD in neuropsychology and was now living in Sacramento, California, where she was working as a researcher at UC Davis University. But she soon left after he got 'too grumpy'.

After finding a 1993 Jerry Hall *Yogacise* DVD in the house he was renting, Michael got into a daily routine of doing 40 minutes of yoga in the morning, speed-walking for 4 miles a day and doing some rope skipping. To his surprise he found he had lots of energy and a focus and strength of mind he had never experienced before. However, halfway through his regime he was no longer losing weight at the same rate, so he dropped his calorie intake down to 600 for the last five weeks, cutting out the bread and having fewer nuts. He eventually lost just over

2 stone in all, dropping from 11.5 stone to reach his target weight of 9st 2lb (58 kg).

'I became almost obsessive. I got to the point where I could walk around a supermarket and know the calorific content of virtually everything on the shelves. I was kind of monk-like. It was like the forty days and forty nights alone in the desert.'

The regime affected him mentally as well as physically. 'It was brutal. When you stop eating, your mind changes. I'd look in the mirror and think I'd gained weight. I had no scales near me or else I'd weigh myself three times a day. I lost my libido completely. I realised that starvation could make you crazy. There's a thin line between control and madness.'

But the discipline of refraining from something that his mind and body were demanding was also enlightening and almost spiritual. 'We live in this society where nowadays if I want something, I take it, I eat it – it's so easy and readily available. When you take all that away, you actually become more appreciative of the things around you.'

Michael forwent his usual visit home to see his parents in Fossa at Christmas. Instead he returned in early January 2008 when the festive feasts and celebrating were over. His parents were shocked by how skinny he looked. 'I remember he was sitting at the bar in the restaurant and I looked at his fingers and I said, "Michael, I think it's enough," Josef recalled. 'After that he went away for another two weeks and what he did then I don't know but he didn't talk to anybody. He didn't want to see anybody.'

When Michael returned to Belfast to resume filming the hunger protest, the cast and crew were as shocked as his parents by his gaunt appearance. It had been Michael's idea to lose so much weight, not the director's, but everyone could now see how much more realistic he would look in playing a man dying from starvation.

The film was structured like a traditional stage play, in three acts. 'I came back with the structure after I went to Belfast for the first time,' Steve explained. 'I suppose I saw the thing as a river. In the first part you are floating on your back, taking in the environment. The second part is like a stretch of rapids – the environment fractures. The third part is like a waterfall – there is this terrible loss of gravity.'

The opening scene shows a man having breakfast at his home in Belfast before going out to his car and checking underneath it for bombs before setting off to work. It is only after some ten minutes that we learn that he is a prison guard. When he enters the Maze, the audience enters with him and follows his working day routine. Dialogue is minimal as new IRA prisoners arrive and, in line with their colleagues, refuse to wear prison uniform in protest at the British government's removal of what was known as Special Category Status for those convicted of political crimes. Knowing that their request to wear their own clothes will be refused, they go naked with just a blanket to cover them and embark on a 'dirty protest' – smearing their cells with their own faeces.

Harrowing scenes of wardens beating inmates and of Michael as Sands being forcefully washed by the wardens and having his hair cut are intertwined with some close-up shots that are oddly beautiful and poetic amid this horror – a fly on a metal grill and even a prison officer's bloodied knuckles as he stands outside in the cleansing snow.

McQueen's pictures paint a thousand words and it is not until the second act, with Michael and Liam Cunningham seated across a desk in the prison visiting room, that there is any real dialogue. The sparky, sometimes humorous, combative conversation comes as something of a relief to viewers who have watched grim, sombre and upsetting scenes of cruelty and endurance. After Sands tells Father Moran that he is intent on a hunger strike to attract more publicity, the final act follows him through his dying days as he gets weaker and starts to hallucinate. Dialogue is minimal once more as the audience is invited to watch his bleak demise. The time for talking is over and Sands is on course for death.

CHAPTER SEVEN

THE GOOD LIFE

After the filming for *Hunger* was completed, Michael had a final health check-up with his doctor to see that he had not harmed himself with the weight loss. 'My doctor said, "Last time you came in here my assistant was outside and she saw you and said, 'My God, that guy's really ill, isn't he?' She thought you had cancer."'

After being given the all clear, he headed to a sushi restaurant in Belfast with Steve McQueen for his first proper meal in months. The small bites suited his condition at a time when his body was not used to handling large amounts of food. But he was freezing cold in the restaurant and wore a thick, padded coat throughout the meal. He ate more sushi than he should have done because he found that he couldn't stop. 'They say your stomach contracts when you cut down on your food intake but I'm not sure I found that to be the case!' he said. 'I ate rather too much sushi than was good for me and, at the end of the meal, I was almost literally laid out cold. It was a weird sensation, like nothing I'd experienced before.'

It took a month's break with Maiko at her apartment in Australia to fully get over his *Hunger* pain. After two weeks he had regained all the weight he had lost and he thoroughly enjoyed the liberty to relax and enjoy himself. 'I felt a huge sense of relief the day after we finished shooting,' he remembered. 'I just wanted to get completely away from *Hunger*, to shake off the role of Bobby Sands and try to get back to some kind of normal life. And I began to appreciate the good things in life more than ever.'

Michael hadn't seen much of Maiko during the filming of *Hunger* so he was pleased to spend some quality time with her in the Australian sunshine as she helped him to relax and get back to normal. 'We ate, we slept, we went to the beach – and those terrible scenes in *Hunger* slowly started to disappear from my mind,' he said.

On 17 February, he and Maiko travelled to Dublin for the annual Irish Film and Television Awards at the Gaiety Theatre. Here he was to present a Best Actress in a Supporting Role Television award to Maria Doyle Kennedy, for her role as Queen Catherine of Aragon in the historical TV drama, *The Tudors*. She was unable to attend, however, so Jonathan Rhys Meyers, who played King Henry VIII, received it in her place. At the after-party revels at the Shelbourne Hotel, Michael was reunited with Liam Cunningham and they enjoyed the company of the likes of Rhys Meyers, Colin Farrell, Victoria Smurfit and Hollywood stars Mel Gibson – recognised with an IFTA award for his Contribution To World Cinema – Rene Russo and Bo Derek.

Later that spring Michael flew out to South Africa to team up again with his *300* co-star Dominic West in a lavish four-part historical drama for Channel 4 called *The Devil's Whore*. It told the story of the English Civil War through the eyes of a spirited 17th-century aristocratic woman named Angelica Fanshawe (Andrea Riseborough). After growing up at a time when the country was both politically and religiously divided, Angelica becomes part of the court of Charles I (Peter Capaldi), enjoying a life of carefree privilege. But England is changing and outside Angelica's gilt-edged world, the people are poor, sick, hungry and angry. And now they are demanding that society and government change radically to ensure a better life for all.

The Royal Family are forced to abandon London and take refuge in Oxford. Finally, the long-threatened war breaks out, with the Royalists and Parliamentarians clashing at the bloody Battle of Edgehill. Finally, the King is put on trial for treason and Oliver Cromwell becomes the first head of the Republican Government.

Michael initially auditioned for the role of the radical anti-monarchist Colonel Edward Sexby but that went to John Simm and he ended up playing the political Roundhead firebrand Thomas Rainsborough. Dominic Wells played Cromwell.

In an official Channel 4 interview for the drama, Michael said,

I knew about Cromwell, having grown up in Ireland. I was aware of the destruction, the way he laid waste to Ireland, and that he was against the Catholic Church, but I didn't actually know much about Charles I and the beheading, and the Roundheads and all the internal politics going on within the revolution.

Rainsborough was almost like Lenin, a radical revolutionary three hundred years before. He wanted to get rid of the monarchy and of the entitlement to vote through nobility and lineage. He felt every man should have the vote, and everybody should be free and should have a say in the running of their country. And Cromwell just thought that was crazy. Rainsborough was quite a dangerous man to have about.

Michael said that his history lessons at school had not taught him about the fighting for social justice during this era. 'I never knew that there was any of this sentiment in seventeenth-century England, with people fighting for the freedom of all men. They just wanted to sweep out the whole system. It would have been very interesting to see what would have happened if they'd got their way.'

The drama was filmed in South Africa, which offered cheaper production costs, and the money saved was put back into the drama. The costumes were particularly sumptuous and the cast was full of admiration for them. 'I'd always thought the Roundheads stuff was a bit uninspiring,' said Dominic West, 'but when you actually put the kit on, all that leather and armour and thigh-length boots, it was just so sexy. You think the Cavaliers have a better look but they don't – they look quite poncey.' West saw the funny side of things too, adding, 'In terms of clanking around in all that armour, I often felt I was in *Carry on Cromwell*. And Monty Python's spectre is never too far away in these things either.'

For his role as Rainsborough, Michael grew his hair down to his shoulders and sported a moustache and goatee beard. On location, he, Simm and West formed a firm alliance, hanging out between breaks, chatting, laughing and recalling old times – more like the Three Musketeers than Puritan Roundheads. 'I had more fun on this than anything I've ever done, mainly because of Michael and John,' said West. 'By the end, we were saying we didn't ever want to do any role again that wasn't on a horse. Sword fights, charging on horseback – it was brilliant, exactly what you always wanted to do from the age of six.'

Michael, as was becoming his custom, took his guitar with him to pass the time in the evenings and on days when he wasn't required for filming but he was enjoying himself so much that John Simm got to play it more than he did himself. 'Michael was out and I'd stay in, strumming away,' Simm joked. 'That's how old I am. It's over!'

The drama was shown in the autumn of 2008 and was well received by viewers and critics. 'What marks this out from your average bodice-ripper is the quality of the acting,' said the *Observer*. 'A rollicking good drama,' agreed the *Guardian*. 'Three loud cheers for *The Devil's Whore*, historical drama as cutting as the lash that bloodies one agitator's back,' said *The Times*.

During one break in filming, Michael flew to Cannes for the film festival in May, when *Hunger* was receiving its world premiere. He was joined by his parents, who watched the screening in some discomfort as their emaciated son portrayed a dying man in prison. Josef later told the Kerry newspaper the *Kingdom*, 'When we saw him in the film, A [Adele] and myself were both so frightened. He looked desperate. But he had to go on a diet as the film would have looked ridiculous if he had not.' But when the film received a standing ovation, they were mightily proud of him and what he had endured for his art. A grinning Michael turned to his father and said, 'It doesn't get any better than this.'

A first-time director, an actor in his first leading role, a grim film with scarce dialogue, subject matter which suggested limited international appeal – it would have challenged any gambler to bet on its odds of success. But in the event *Hunger* won the coveted Camera d'Or for Best First Feature.

After being presented with the award, Steve McQueen said, 'My film was about The Troubles in Northern Ireland during the 1981 hunger strikes. Within the prison, there were prison officers who I identify with and protestors who I identify with. The film is about people in a situation and what these people do. Thank you very much.'

The film's co-producer Laura Hastings-Smith thought the story went beyond the prison walls to strike a chord with everyone around the world. 'We're all absolutely thrilled, and thrilled for Steve, thrilled for the film and for everyone who's worked on *Hunger*,' she said. 'The key to the film was that it looked at the humanity of the story and how this place, Maze Prison, at that time in history, was a brutalising place for everyone – be you prison officer, prisoner, orderly or riot guard. It was a tragedy for everyone. We looked at what happens when dialogue stops and that has a resonance across the world.'

After the most unpromising of initial meetings, Michael and Steve had forged an unlikely alliance, friendship and respect. Both had been on escalating career paths to fame but now they stood on the brink of international acclaim and stardom. Life for both of them would change immeasurably.

Hunger may have had the look of an art-house film – slow paced, beautifully shot, minimal dialogue – but Steve McQueen baulked at such a notion. 'What I tried to do was make the strongest, most powerful film I could from the events and the story. It may not have the conventional narrative of most feature films but that is my way of grappling with the subject. Art has absolutely nothing to do with it,' he told the *Observer*. 'What initially brought me to the subject was the notion of what an individual is capable of doing just in order to be heard. People say, "Oh, it's a political film," but for me it's essentially about what we, as humans, are capable of, morally, physically, psychologically. What we will inflict and what we can endure.'

And to *Dazed & Confused* magazine, he explained, 'Film-making is very much about telling stories. Whether I make art or films, it's about engaging the audience.' He rejected the suggestion that his film set out to portray Sands as a martyr but said it was ultimately uplifting. 'The movie is a journey through H Block. You are focusing on the things you find interesting. You follow prison officers. You follow a hunger striker. A prison officer's routine is just that: routine. But what happens to Bobby Sands is quite extraordinary. Obviously, as a storyteller, you follow that. I am not a nationalist. I am not a unionist. The human element overrides all that nonsense. Before you are Irish or British, you are a human being.'

Michael also stressed that the film was non-partisan. 'To balance all that [prisoner cruelty] we show an IRA man gunning down a prison officer in cold blood, in a nursing home in front of his own mother and a room full of elderly residents,' he said. 'What I like about the film is you look at it and it's not about a political thing, it's about how people treat each other, and how people can be cruel to each and how that affects them as well.'

Both the director and his leading man had much praise for each other. In an interview with the *Hollywood Reporter*, Steve expressed just how much he admired Michael's talent as an actor. 'He's a game-changer. He's got a vulnerability and sensuality that is very powerful. He's got an extraordinary femininity while still being very much a man's man. That's what propels him to greater roles. Often with leading actors, there's a place they go, but they don't go all the way. There are actors and there are artists, and Michael is an artist.'

Michael reciprocated by enthusing about the experience of working with Steve. 'Everything about him was a real joy,' he said. 'He certainly brought out the best of me. It's definitely the best work I've done to date and a lot of that's down to him. He's a pretty extraordinary person to work with.'

Michael knew that *Hunger* would be a life-changing experience and he was truly grateful to be cast in the film.

'For somebody to take such a risk and give me the opportunity to do that was massive,' he was later to recall. 'In terms of me breaking into film and leading-man roles in film, *Hunger*, for sure, changed my life.'

He also revealed that the 'faeces' smeared over the cell walls was actually chocolate mousse – 'I could have wiped a bit off and eaten it!'

Michael's rapport with Liam Cunningham had developed into a friendship that was to last and he felt fortunate to have been working with him. 'Liam and I had a great relationship when we were making the film and it was so important for our scene together,' he said.

While in Cannes he disclosed that he would be playing Heathcliff in a new movie version of Emily Bronte's classic love story, *Wuthering Heights*. It was to be directed by John Maybury, who had directed *The Jacket* and *The Edge of Love*, both featuring Keira Knightley. 'I'm very curious who they will cast as Cathy,' Michael told reporters. 'Heathcliff is a great role but I'm a bit nervous about it until I get my Yorkshire accent right.' Pretty Australian actress Abbie Cornish, who had starred in *Somersault*, *Bright Star* and *Sucker Punch*, was later cast as Cathy.

After his success at Cannes, a joyous Michael bid farewell to his parents and flew back out to South Africa to complete filming on *The Devil's Whore*. It was then that he was telephoned by Andrea Arnold, a former children's-TV presenter turned director, who wanted him to be in her new movie, *Fish Tank*. It was only her second feature-length movie. Her first, *Red Road,* had focused on a female CCTV operator on a Glasgow housing estate who spots a face from the past on her monitor – one she had hoped she would never see again. She becomes obsessed with finding out more about this man so she follows him, stalker-like, in real life and on CCTV. The tension builds as viewers wonder what the connection is between the two but it is not until the end that the shocking truth is revealed. The film won several awards, including the Prix du Jury in Cannes in 2006 and the Carl Foreman Award at the British Academy Awards. A previous short, *Wasp*, had won an Oscar in 2005 for Best Live Action Short.

Andrea gave Michael the concept of *Fish Tank* and told him the role she wanted him to play but not a full synopsis or even what would happen at the end because she did not want her cast to know the whole story. Michael had seen and enjoyed *Red Road* and he accepted the role without having read the script. They were to be given their lines in sections only a few days before filming them.

Andrea had not seen or even heard of *Hunger* when she first thought of Michael for the role. She remembered him from the Irvine Welsh film, *Wedding Belles*, in which she considered him to be 'very charismatic', and made the decision to approach him without meeting him. 'He felt right and I trust my instincts that way. I don't like to question myself when it feels right, so I just went for it,' she was to explain.

In the summer of 2008 Michael began working on the film. The story revolved around the life of a volatile 15-year-old girl named Mia, living on a council estate in Essex with her single mother, Joanne, and foul-mouthed younger sister, Tyler. Mia is a loner who has been excluded from school and ostracised by her friends. Her only source of escape is hip-hop dance, which she practises alone.

One hot summer's day her mother, Joanne (Kierston Wareing), brings home her boyfriend Connor, played by Michael, who appears to be a charming and handsome Irishman. He encourages Mia in her dancing and persuades her to send a video tape to a local club that is looking for dancers. One evening after drinking together, the pair have sex while Joanne is asleep upstairs. He tells her to keep it secret. When Michael splits with Joanne and returns to his own home, Mia tracks him down and discovers he is married with a daughter. Later, at the dance auditions, she discovers they are looking for erotic dancers so she walks away.

Andrea was keen to cast as many non-actors as possible – including the part of Mia. 'I wanted someone who would give me trouble for real. I wanted a girl who would not have to act, could just be herself,' she explained. She spotted 17-year-old Katie Jarvis at Tilbury train station in Essex, arguing with her boyfriend. When Andrea approached her, Katie didn't believe she was wanted for a film and refused to hand over her telephone number. But eventually she was persuaded. 'She came from where we were going to film and felt very real,' said Andrea.

The role of Connor was also originally to be played by a non-actor. Andrea had her eye on a man she used to see in her local park emptying the bins, who she thought would be perfect for the part. 'But then I began to think it would be interesting to have someone with experience mixed in with Katie's innocence, as that would echo the relationship in the film and could work well,' she explained.

For an actor who likes to prepare fully and work on a character's background story for all his roles, Michael found Andrea's working procedure – in which she fed the scripts to the cast in piecemeal fashion – to be a challenge, but one he was willing to face. 'Not having a script is kind of worrying and most of the time you wouldn't commit to something under those circumstances, but I'd seen *Red Road* and I really respected Andrea and wanted to work with her,' he said. 'I find her storytelling very interesting because it's in the grey area. She deals with human beings who have flaws and have good qualities and negative qualities and are basically just trying to figure their way through life.'

Michael liked the fact that Andrea was non-judgemental of her characters and their actions and decisions. 'There's no clear right or wrong. Connor does cross the line but, on the flipside, he is the catalyst for Mia to become her own person. He is the only one who inspires her with confidence to follow her dreams. And that she's not destined for shit. And so it's again playing with that ambiguity.'

Andrea, he thought, shared with Quentin Tarantino and Steve McQueen a passion and perfectionist quality when it came to film-making. 'There's a level of commitment that they bring and they expect everybody else to bring that with them when they come to work. And they're very clear communicators of what they're looking for. Therefore, it becomes very easy to trust them and give yourself up to them, to push you beyond your safety net and your safety zone.'

For her part, Andrea admired Michael for giving up his usual working procedure and for having faith in her and the movie, which was shot over just six weeks in Essex. 'It was brave of him to do this film really because I didn't show him or anyone in the film the script beforehand so he didn't know what he was letting himself in for. I wanted to shoot in order, so that the story would reveal itself to everyone as we went along.'

Although feeling out of his comfort zone, Michael got to enjoy this unusual way of working. He enjoyed the element of improvisation and found it challenging and rewarding. 'We didn't rehearse, talk much about anything, we just worked on every day as it came,' he recalled. 'I usually like to digest the script and let it rot and then play with it when it comes to the day of filming, so in this instance I tried to be as loose and relaxed as possible. That was the main note I gave myself. Andrea is very quick and off the cuff, and works with whatever happens that day to organically feed her story and creates a very comfortable space for the actors to work in.'

Kierston Wareing was more used to such a flexible working practice. She had made her feature-film debut in Ken Loach's *It's a Free World*, in which she starred as Angie who, after being fired from her 30th job for bad behaviour, sets up an unregistered recruitment agency with her flatmate, Rose, which they run from their kitchen. 'I love Andrea's way of shooting – that's how I worked with Ken Loach, so it was great to have the opportunity to do it again,' she said. 'In some ways I think it was good, not telling us the story in advance, because you try and put the story together in your head yourself and bit by bit I was slowly working it out.'

Kierston appreciated what she considered to be Michael's humility. 'Michael is so down to earth and lovely and normal. There wasn't a barrier in terms of his film experience versus anyone else's,' she said.

Young Katie, who had never acted before, also found him friendly and supportive. 'He gave me advice about certain things and was really helpful,' she said. 'It felt a bit weird acting some scenes with him but, because I knew what he was like off camera, it made it much easier.'

The filming experience was also made easier for Michael because of the bond he made with his co-stars. 'It was great working with Kierston,' he recalled. 'She's very no-nonsense and when I first saw her I thought she looked like

Brigitte Bardot. She's got this very interesting quality to her – she's got this sultry, sexy rawness to her and she's very free and easy to work with. I watched *It's a Free World* while we were working and saw how talented she is. She's also fun.'

Michael thought that Andrea's working method also brought out the best in Katie, tapping into her natural behaviour. 'Katie is a very expressive person and very easy to play with as she's not really acting. In Andrea's hands you can get a very powerful performance in that way as it's very raw, it comes from the gut, it hasn't been overthought, it's very intuitive.'

In an interview with *Under the Radar* magazine, Michael talked about the excitement of staying flexible and open during filming and not adhering too strictly to what you have planned in your head. 'Say you're breaking up with somebody. It doesn't always have to be tears and screaming. It can also be funny moments and understanding or whatever,' he explained. 'It's just kinda freeing yourself up and being relaxed to allow whatever comes in on the day, to not try and block things. In your rehearsal period and your preparation, you have an idea of where it's going to go but that doesn't mean, on the day, it goes that way. Something might happen to you that day. You might get some bad news. To allow it to seep into what you're doing, I think, is all right, because different things happen in people's lives for real that will colour your interpretation or your reaction to something. So, I think just keeping it alive and being relaxed is the most important thing.'

Finally, it was during the filming of *Fish Tank* that Michael heard, to his amazement, that his agent had arranged for him to audition for one of his teenage heroes, who was due to shoot a blockbuster World War II movie starring one of Hollywood's biggest names.

CHAPTER EIGHT

CONFESSING
TO TARANTINO

Michael had assumed that Quentin Tarantino had seen him in *Hunger* but, in fact, he had yet to see the movie. But Michael's agent had been pestering the director to see Michael for a role in his new, oddly spelt movie, *Inglourious Basterds*.

Hollywood A-lister Brad Pitt had the lead role of Aldo, leader of a fearsome band of Jewish fighters, known as The Basterds, who exact their revenge on the Nazis in France, spreading fear by killing and scalping them. Michael was sent the script and was told there were two roles that required actors who could speak English and German fluently. One was the sinister but smiling Nazi Colonel Hans Landa and the other was British officer, Lt. Archie

Hicox, who goes on an undercover mission in Nazi-occupied France. Michael was told to prepare for both roles but, because he was working on *Fish Tank*, he didn't have time to learn both so he focused on Landa. He spent a day rehearsing an audition piece before flying out to Berlin, where the film was being shot, to meet Tarantino.

He was nervous, particularly because Tarantino plays all the other parts when auditioning actors. Things were to get ever hairier when he arrived. 'Quentin and I chatted for a bit, then he said, "OK, let's take a look at Hicox,"' Michael told the *Sunday Times*. 'I was like, "What about Landa?" And he goes, "Well, I cast my Landa on Tuesday." "Are you sure?" "Yeah, I'm sure, man." Then there was a pause and he goes, "Look, man, any guy that gets cast as Heathcliff is not fucking German enough to play my Landa, all right?" And I thought, "I'm not going to argue with Quentin Tarantino about who he wants to cast, that's for sure."'

So Michael took a deep breath and began reading for Hicox but, after he was done, Quentin told him that he was sounding like Michael Caine and that he wasn't looking for that. So Michael had another go, this time giving it his best English stiff upper lip. The director thanked him and Michael left, feeling despondent. 'I thought I'd made a balls of the audition, to be honest, and I was totally depressed when I left.' But to his amazement, a week later he was offered the part.

Only then did Quentin tell him that he was looking for

'a young George Sanders'. Michael was not familiar with the urbane English actor with the rich, cultured English accent. He had co-starred with the likes of Bette Davis and Laurence Olivier during the 1940s and 1950s in *All About Eve* and *Rebecca,* and was the voice of the imperious-sounding tiger Shere Khan in Walt Disney's *Jungle Book.* He was usually cast as a cad or villain – often both – but he had also played the heroic Simon Templar, aka The Saint, in several movies.

Quentin sent Michael several DVDs of his movies to watch, including those of *The Saint*, and he finally understood what the director was looking for. 'That's where I got most of my inspiration, trying to concentrate on the clipped way he spoke and the rhythms and the colours of it. And that physicality – the way he carried himself and held a cigarette or a glass of whisky. Everything was like a sort of foreplay. I really wanted to encapsulate that. And I found some humour in the character.'

Michael may not have thought highly of his original audition with Quentin but Lawrence Bender, who had produced *Reservoir Dogs*, *Pulp Fiction* and *Jackie Brown* for the director, and was producing *Inglorious Basterds*, certainly did. 'There were a lot of people being considered for that role,' he recalled, 'including some big actors. But he [Michael] was a powerhouse. He just knocked us out. It's such a wonderful thing to watch an actor take control of the room.' Quentin was pleased that he had not only found a fine actor in Michael but that he also spoke excellent German.

Meanwhile, *Hunger* received its London premiere on 19 October as part of the London Film Festival at the Leicester Square Odeon. A rather tired-looking Michael arrived, along with the cast and director, and the film received rapturous applause. The critics' reviews were effusive. The *Independent* called *Hunger* 'a stunning, uniquely powerful film' and the *Daily Telegraph* praised Steve McQueen for a 'sensational feature debut, fearless and uncompromising, bolder than any film to come out of the UK in a long time'.

Michael's own reviews were the kind that he might have dreamed of as a struggling actor. 'Michael Fassbender gives an extraordinary performance as Bobby Sands in a gruelling picture of immense power and beauty,' said the *Daily Express*. 'At its centre, *Hunger* features an extraordinary performance by the young German-Irish actor Michael Fassbender as Bobby Sands,' agreed the *Observer*. 'An icily brilliant and superbly acted film,' said the *Guardian*, adding, 'Fassbender gives another ferociously convincing performance.'

The Times singled out the Fassbender/Cunningham scene as a 'breathtaking centrepiece of a film that is both politically controversial and philosophically sublime.' Its critic said that the two actors had provided 'a master class in screen acting from two very different performers'.

All the reviews were immensely satisfying to the team and a great relief but Michael was still nervous about what he considered the most daunting prospect of all – the movie's premiere in Belfast the following day. Despite rumours that there would be a protest outside the Movie House cinema where the film was to be screened, in the event there were none and the film received a warm reception from most of the audience. But it did not please everyone. Some unionists thought it biased towards the republicans but Michael was pleased when a security guard took him aside at the after-show party to express his surprise that the film was such a human story. 'That's your average punter who's going to go and see the film, and when somebody like that says it, I was like, "OK, the message is pretty clear,"' Michael said later.

Feeling that the screening had gone as well as he could have hoped and having relaxed at the after-show party, a relieved Michael invited his family – parents, aunts, uncles, cousins who were in attendance – back to his hotel for a celebration drink. This went on until 5am and, when he awoke a few hours later, it was to face an interview with the *Guardian*. Cradling a Bloody Mary, he told the paper, 'Everybody I spoke to here, every family, has some connection with The Troubles one way or another and it's still an open wound. I mean, I've seen so many films about The Troubles that I've found insulting.'

But as he had hoped, *Hunger*'s message was pretty clear. The *Irish Times* said, 'This haunting, boldly unconventional film plays on in the mind well after it's over, as we ponder what we have seen and the issues it raises.' The *Belfast Telegraph* described it as a 'harrowing, brilliant film' and said of Michael, 'Few actors get a defining role so early in their film career but Michael Fassbender has done just that with his powerful performance as the IRA prisoner Bobby Sands.'

Above all, Michael was enjoying the experience of taking on challenging roles that would push him and excite him. But, influenced by another childhood hero, John Cazale, he was interested in emotionally complex characters rather than heroic lead roles. When asked by *Anthem* magazine whether he was attracted to controversial ones, having played Bobby Sands in *Hunger* and the predatory Connor in *Fish Tank*, he replied, 'It's definitely important for me to keep challenging myself and take risks. That's the most exciting thing about my job. I just want to learn as much as I can. I definitely like to do things that scare me a little bit but I don't necessarily seek them out.'

Michael enjoyed his experience with Steve McQueen so much that he was eager to work with him in the future. 'I said to Steve, "If you ever want to work together again and I'm around, here's my card!"' Towards the end of the year he and Steve met again when they were among those invited to a function at the Houses of Parliament in celebration of Film Four, who had made *Hunger*. Over dinner, Steve told him the premise of a new film he was planning about a sex addict. Michael was surprised because Steve had earlier suggested that his next project might be a love story. But the more Steve talked about it, the more Michael began to think it was a subject ripe for a movie. 'It seemed obvious to me after he had mentioned it,' he recalled, 'because the media at the time was taking a look at sexual addiction because of some celebrity element, but the film world hadn't really tackled it. And knowing Steve, I knew it was going to be pretty uncompromising.'

The idea had, in fact, come from playwright and screenwriter Abi Morgan, who had written the Channel 4 TV movie *Sex Traffic*. Intrigued by *Hunger*, Abi sought out a meeting with Steve McQueen and the pair met in a café. Each of them only had an hour to spare but they ended up talking for three and a half. 'We had a discussion that started off about the Internet, then it went on to pornography, then we got on to sex addiction,' Steve recalled. 'Abi's amazing. It was a situation where she immediately felt like a friend I'd known for a long, long time. The second time we met, in a restaurant, we'd written the first twenty minutes of the script by the end of the conversation.'

Michael felt intuitively that whatever movie Steve was planning he needed to be in it. 'Things changed for me after *Hunger* and to have the opportunity at that time to do something like that with somebody like him... it felt like we'd sort of formed a union then. So whatever it was, I was going to be involved with him if he wanted to have me.'

In the meantime, Michael had to prepare for *Inglourious Basterds*. His character, Hicox, goes undercover as a German officer as part of a mission to assassinate the leaders of the Third Reich and, although Michael can chat in German, his diction needed working on. So, to avoid speaking German with an English accent, he worked with a vocal coach to prepare for the role.

Filming got underway on 9 October but Michael, who only had a couple of scenes in the film, was not required until a few weeks later. The production team arranged his flight tickets to Berlin but Michael declined, saying he would make his own way there. The senior production crew were startled to discover that this meant travelling across Europe on his beloved motorbike, a Triumph Speed Triple. Worried that one of their key actors might injure himself on such a powerful machine, they forbade him to ride it until filming was over.

Perhaps it was his Catholic upbringing but Michael felt that he needed to confess to Quentin about something from his past. During a quiet moment in Berlin, he took the opportunity to admit that when he was 18 he had not only put on a production of *Reservoir Dogs* in a Killarney nightclub, but that he had directed and starred in it as Mr Pink, without asking permission for the copyright. To his relief, the director wasn't concerned when Michael pointed out that the profit went to a good cause and that none of those involved in the production made any personal financial gain. 'He was happy once I assured him that the proceeds went to charity,' Michael told the *Irish Times*. Michael has since re-told this story in several broadcast interviews and does a decent impression of the director's fast and breathless voice with the line, 'Well, as long as nobody made any money out of it.'

Inglourious Basterds was shot almost entirely in sequence, beginning with a tense and powerful scene in which Landa visits the French farmer Lapadite's house. Landa is seemingly all charm and manners but there is a chilling undercurrent that ultimately leads to Lapadite betraying the Jews he is hiding under his floorboards, in order to save his own family.

The dialogue and the thrilling, scary sense of foreboding was Quentin Tarantino at his best and was replicated an hour into the film in a scene between the undercover Hicox and another Nazi officer, Major Hellstrom, in a French bistro. Hellstrom overhears Hicox talking and is suspicious of his accent. He swaggers over to join him and his co-conspirators at the table, sharing a drink and playing a pub game. But, as with Landa, there is a menace about him that is not far from the surface and again the tension mounts in a game of cat-and-mouse, developing into a Mexican stand-off with both men aiming pistols under the table at each other's crotches.

Michael was fascinated by the way that Quentin would

sometimes close his eyes during the filming of a scene with a lot of dialogue so as to concentrate on the rhythm of the language 'like a piece of music'. He was also impressed by Quentin's almost encyclopaedic knowledge and casual references to even the most unknown of movies and TV shows. 'You could mention the most obscure Egyptian film from like nineteen-fucking-thirty-three, and he'll have seen it, and he'll tell you scenes of the film that he liked or didn't like. It's just astounding,' he recalled.

The two amused themselves when not filming by quizzing each other on film and television. Michael eventually stumped his opponent with a question going back to his childhood love of American TV shows. 'I got him when I asked what the names of the two Dobermanns on the 1980s series *Magnum, P.I* [were],' he recalled. 'They were Apollo and Zeus. I was pretty pleased with myself.'

As for his fellow cast members, Michael admitted to the *Belfast Telegraph* that he had convinced himself he would dislike Brad Pitt but that they ended up forming a strong bond. 'I really wanted to hate him but he's a nice guy and very encouraging. The fame doesn't affect him. He just comes and does his work. He's a real person and very focused.'

Working with such luminaries did make Michael nervous though. As he told Irish TV chat-show host Ryan Tubridy, 'It's just mad to be standing on set with Brad Pitt there doing his stuff and Quentin in the corner. I'm kind of like, "Hang on a second. I'm from Killarney!" But then you get over it and off you go.'

During filming, the producer, Lawrence Bender, was visited by his former girlfriend, Suni 'Leasi' Andrews, and their two-year-old daughter. Suni had played a character called Danya in a US TV supernatural drama called *Dante's Cove*. Michael, who had split up with Maiko Spencer, was taken with her beauty and a romance ensued.

Filming wrapped in December in time for the Cannes Film Festival the following May. Michael received high praise from Quentin – 'Michael's like an old-style British actor from the forties – he's got the grace and the looks. I would love to work with him again.'

Inglourious Basterds was a big movie on Michael's career path but he had no time to settle back and enjoy his moment. Instead, he was determined to keep moving while the going was good.

'I don't know what's going to happen. I'm flavour of the month at the moment but somebody else is going to roll around the corner in three months' time. I just want to keep working. I can't stop!' he told the *Guardian*.

Asked by the *Belfast Telegraph* if he was worried about the increased public attention he might get after a Tarantino movie, he replied, 'I don't think people really recognise me, to be honest. I just take each day as it comes.

'I'm very happy to be observing and not be observed. I can sit in a café and watch people – I'm happier doing that. But the pros definitely outweigh the cons in this game. It's such a privileged line of work, you can't really complain about anything.'

Shortly after finishing work on *Inglourious Basterds*, Michael starred in a short movie called *Man on a Motorcycle*, written and directed by a former musician with the Scottish group The Beta Band, John Maclean. Michael's agent, Conor McCaughan, was a friend of his and was impressed by the music videos he had made for his other band, The Aliens. Conor introduced John to Michael, who had also admired his videos. John was progressing into short movies and when Michael offered to appear in one, a delighted John quickly wrote *Man On a Motorcycle,* which he said was based around Michael's availability and 'what he would probably find fun to do'.

Man on a Motorcycle was so low-budget that it was filmed on a camera phone and involved a week of shooting a motorcycle courier around London. Another actor filmed those scenes wearing a crash helmet but when he took off the helmet it was edited to show Michael. The clever technique meant that he was only required for one day of filming, which was just as well, for he was about to become very busy collecting awards.

CHAPTER NINE

AND THE WINNER IS...

On 11 January 2009 Michael attended the New York Film Critics Circle Awards, where he saw Steve McQueen win Best First Feature for *Hunger*. There was more personal success, though, at the London Film Critics Circle Awards, held at the Grosvenor House Hotel on 4 February, where Michael won British Actor of the Year in an impressive category that listed Ralph Fiennes, Ben Kingsley, Michael Sheen and Dev Patel. Steve McQueen won the Breakthrough British Film-maker award.

The annual whirlwind of awards ceremonies saw Michael at the BAFTAs on 8 February, where he was nominated in the Rising Star category but lost out to Noel Clarke. *Hunger* also lost to *Man on Wire* for

Outstanding British Film, but Steve picked up the Special Achievement award for his first feature film. Six days later Michael was back in Ireland for the IFTAs at the Burlington Hotel, Dublin.

Michael had been dividing his time between his home in Hackney, east London, hotels around the world and Leasi Andrews' house in Bel Air, Los Angeles. While in LA, his pilates teacher reintroduced him to his boyhood pastime of archery and he frequented the Rancho Park Archery Range on Motor Avenue with her, her husband and Leasi. Another favourite LA pastime was browsing at Book Soup, a bookshop on Sunset Boulevard. He particularly enjoyed reading one of his favourite authors, Hunter S. Thompson, whose journalistic style appealed to him. But it wasn't all living the Hollywood dream. Michael had to get his hands dirty one day when there was a problem with the plumbing and, in his words, he spent a couple of days 'literally mopping up shit' before it was fixed.

Whenever asked about his love life by journalists, the usually talkative Michael politely declined to furnish any details. But Leasi accompanied him to the IFTAs, where she met his family and friends and watched him being honoured by his homeland on a victorious night. *Hunger* had been nominated in eight categories and swept the board with six awards, including Best Film, Best Actor for Michael, Best Supporting Actor for Liam Cunningham, Original Score, Production Design and Sound. In addition, Michael received the Rising Star award and was also nominated for Best Supporting Actor in television for *The Devil's Whore*.

Michael expressed his delight and relief that all the hard work involved in playing Bobby Sands and the concern over the sensitive nature of the story had ultimately paid off, given the international acclaim that *Hunger* had received. 'There were times when I questioned what I was doing to myself but the people involved in the film, who were so passionate and talented, kept me strong,' he said. 'Now for the film to have received so many awards and nods from our peers in the industry makes all the effort worthwhile. I'm just so glad that it has done so well and has got the recognition that I believe it truly deserved.

'I guess that no matter what else happens in my career from here on I can always say I had this amazingly successful night and this fantastic film where I can say, "I did that, I achieved something great."'

He later joked to reporters that he was surprised to win the Rising Star award. 'I've been doing this for over ten years so I wonder why I'm still getting Rising Star awards, but it's great to get it in Ireland, which is where I consider home.'

Hunger was overlooked for the Oscars but Michael won a consolation Best Actor at the Kermode Awards in London on 17 February. Hosted by the BBC film critic, Mark Kermode, the light-hearted event rewards those who have been overlooked by the Oscars and Michael turned up cheerfully to accept his honour.

During the filming of *Inglourious Basterds*, Michael had signed up for the lead role in director Neil Marshall's new movie, *Centurion*. The story centred on the historical event where the elite Ninth Roman legion disappeared without trace after entering Scotland to do battle with the Picts. On the way back from Berlin, after filming of *Basterds* had wrapped, Michael got talking to an amateur historian and told him about the project. But he was taken aback by the man's succinct reply. 'He said, "Yeah, that's bullshit. They were nowhere near Scotland,"' Michael told *The Times*. 'But it didn't put me off!'

Michael was cast as the centurion Quintus Dias who, during the Roman conquest of Britain in the second century, led a group of soldiers on a raid of a Pictish camp to rescue a captured general, played by Michael's *300* colleague, Dominic West. But when the son of the Pictish leader is murdered during the raid, the Romans find themselves hunted by a seemingly unstoppable group of the Picts' most vicious and skilled warriors, led by a beautiful and deadly tracker (*Quantum Of Solace* actress Olga Kurylenko) and hell-bent on revenge.

By now Michael was used to changing his body shape to play a role – be it losing weight or bulking up – and he took to the gym once more to play a very muscular-looking Quintus. 'I'm lucky I take after my mum's side of the family and have a really fast metabolism,' he has said. 'When I do get into the gym whenever possible, I tend to do boxing training. Jump rope, focus mitts, heavy bag, push-ups, reps, high intensity.'

Filming took place in the Highlands of Scotland in February 2009 in freezing temperatures with snow, ice, wind and rain. The very first day of shooting turned out to be the biggest trial for the cast and they wondered what they had let themselves in for. They had to make their way to a peak near Inverness using specially adapted Norwegian Army snowmobiles to transport them in sub-zero temperatures, with the actors wearing authentic thin Roman tunics and only overcoats for extra protection against the elements. Once there they had to tramp through two feet of snow with bare arms and legs as the cameras rolled. 'It was pretty cold but you knew what you were getting on screen was going to look pretty impressive,' said Michael.

Fortunately for the cast, Neil Marshall works very fast so they didn't need to do many takes. 'There wasn't too much acting to do on the part of the actors,' he said. 'They got up there in their Roman outfits. They've got bare arms and they were absolutely freezing. So they were genuinely clinging close to keep warm. When they're shivering on screen, it's real. I wanted that.'

Among the health and safety notes handed out to the crew was a telling sentence which read, 'Actors are subject to risk of cold-water shock, hypothermia, water inhalation and drowning.' The temperature dropped to minus 18°C that day and Noel Clarke, who played a centurion, got frostbite. In one scene, Michael is on the run from the Picts with a handful of his soldiers, played by David Morrissey, Dimitri Leonidas and his *Hunger* colleague, Liam Cunningham. They drift down an icy river before hauling themselves ashore. At the end of a day's filming their favourite warming meal was a hot curry.

Despite the ordeal, Michael enjoyed shooting another action adventure, which required a lot of running, riding, sword fights and litres of blood as killings and decapitations abound. But he had to be dissuaded from undertaking one of the boldest stunts in the movie – jumping from a high-sided gorge into the deep, rushing water. Neil Marshall was full of admiration for Michael. 'He is absolutely dedicated,' he recalled. 'He's up for anything, whether it's jumping into an icy, cold river or getting on a horse and riding at high speed. I'm sure if I'd said yes he would have jumped off the cliff into the river but somebody had to hold him back and say, "No, no, no – let's not get carried away here!"'

Michael liked the pace of the film and Neil's no-nonsense approach. 'Neil is one of those directors who really enjoys what he's doing,' he told the *Independent*. 'There's no fuss. It's bang, bang, bang. He moves at a pace and he's happy to be on set every day. He loves shooting entertaining films.'

The part of Quintus intrigued Michael. 'We know that Quintus's father was a famous gladiator who won his freedom in the Coliseum. I thought that was quite interesting – somebody who lives in the shadow of his father and feels like he's got a lot to prove. As the film progresses, he's thrown into a position of command. I thought it was quite interesting to play with his doubts and the journey of the man – how he actually steps up to the plate and takes command. We know at the beginning he's very much for the ethos of Rome; he totally believes in it. But as the film moves on he becomes disillusioned with the Roman Empire.'

The movie received mixed reviews, although even the better ones generally thought the characters were one-dimensional or, at worst, unbelievable. 'Rousing if slightly predictable,' said *Variety*. 'An entertaining if uneven historical drama that starts stronger than it finishes,' griped *Total Film*. 'Energetic, relentless and tipping towards monotony,' commented the *Guardian*. 'A gritty, brutal chase movie that's more about swords (and spears, and axes) than sandals – although it could have done with a lot more character-meat on those bones,' complained *Empire*.

At least Michael received some kinder words. 'The fearless, credible Fassbender deserves better than this,' insisted *Time Out*, and the *Financial Times* was impressed by his performance. 'He shines. There is a nice seriousness to Fassbender – he looks utterly humourless – and has the remove and weird separateness of a young William Hurt.'

Meanwhile, the *Wuthering Heights* project had failed to

get off the ground. A new director, Peter Webber, took over the project in May 2009, casting Gemma Arterton and Ed Westwick in the lead roles, but this version, too, failed to achieve lift-off. Angela Arnold eventually took over in January 2010, using Kaya Scodelario and James Howson as her Heathcliff and Cathy.

So, in June 2009, Michael – having enjoyed his romp as a Roundhead in *The Devil's Whore* – chose to fulfil another boyhood dream by appearing in a Western. Jonah Hex is a DC Comics character created by John Albano and Tony DeZuniga, and first appeared in *All-Star Western* magazine in 1972. A violent, facially scarred bounty hunter, he roams the American western frontier in the 19th century, having battled alcoholism and dealing with his mother turning to prostitution.

In the movie version, Jonah is a Confederate cavalryman during the Civil War. He is ordered by his commanding officer, General Quentin Turnbull, to burn down a hospital but Jonah refuses and is forced to kill his best friend, Turnbull's son Jeb. After the war, a vengeful Turnbull and his right-hand man, Burke – a psychotic who takes pleasure in torture and killing – tie Jonah up and force him to watch as his house is burned down with his wife and son inside. Turnbull then brands Jonah's face with his initials, QT, and leaves him to die. He escapes and turns to bounty hunting but when a sheriff refuses to pay him for bringing in four dead outlaws and plans to kill him instead, Jonah shoots him and his deputies and takes the

chael Fassbender arriving for the 2012 Golden Globes in Los Angeles.

Above: Life out of the *Fish Tank*, at the Cannes Festival in 2009, Fassbender with direct Andrea Arnold.

Below: An *Inglourious* knees-up with *Basterds* co-stars Fassbender, Brad Pitt, Diane Kruger and Mélanie Laurent, with director Quentin Tarantino second-right.

rey Mulligan had first appeared with Fassbender in TV's *Trial & Retribution*. They
er reunited as *Shame*'s siblings.

Above: *Shame* producers Emile Sherman and Iain Canning with Fassbender and direct
Steve McQueen.

Below: Fassbender in September 2011 with the Best Actor award for *Shame* at the Venice
Film Festival. '*Buona sera, Venezia,*' said Fassbender in his acceptance speech. '*Grazie mil*

Left: Fassbender and Antonio Banderas both made appearances in Steven Soderbergh's *Haywire*.

Below: A young looking Ian McKellen and Patrick Stewart – aka their younger selves as played by Fassbender and James McAvoy the *X-Men: First Class*.

Above: Fassbender with *Jane Eyre* co-star and director Mia Wasikowska and Cary Fukuna

Below left: *Prometheus* co-stars Fassbender and Charlize Theron.

Below right: *Dangerous Method* acting with Kiera Knightly and Viggo Mortensen.

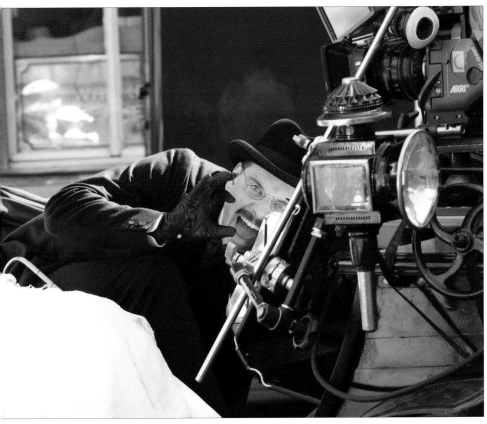

ove: Old cronies – David Cronenberg directed *A Dangerous Method*.

ow: The doctor will see you now – *A Dangerous Method*.

Michael Fassbender at *The Daily Show* studios in June 2012.

money owed him. Meanwhile, a very much alive Turnbull is planning a terrorist attack for 4 July during the celebration of the American centennial. The US Army makes a deal with Jonah to track down and kill Turnbull in exchange for his freedom.

Filming of *Jonah Hex* began in Louisiana in April 2009 with Josh Brolin in the title role, Megan Fox playing his love interest – a gun-wielding prostitute called Lilah – John Malkovich as Turnbull and Michael as Burke – a bowler-hatted, tattooed Irishman. 'It was a trip, really, because it was a Western in one sense and then a comic book in another and we just sort of went all out and had as much fun with it as we could, and didn't get stuck in any genre,' Michael told an audience at Comic Con in San Diego, California, in July 2009. 'It's all boys with toys and cowboy costumes – a dream come true.'

Michael took his inspiration from *A Clockwork Orange* when it came to wearing the bowler. He couldn't quite figure out the character of Burke until he went to the costume designer and found a bowler hat, which he tried on. 'Once I put the bowler hat on, I channelled Burke through that,' he said. 'Burke is Irish but he's ended up in America so I always thought he was running away from something in his past. He's an opportunist. He's a mercenary first and foremost. His weapon of choice is a Bowie knife and he likes to kill fresh prostitutes. That's where he gets his kicks.'

Michael also referenced some of the crazed personality

of Frank Gorshin's portrayal of The Riddler in the 1960s *Batman* TV series. Initially he was asked to wear a lurid green three-piece suit but he baulked at the outfit and asked them to tone down the green or he would be a laughing stock back home in Ireland! It was eventually muted into a muddy green/brown suit and grey shirt.

The film, directed by Jimmy Hayward, was a huge flop – shunned by movie-goers and panned by critics. The *San Francisco Chronicle* was succinct – 'A plot would have been nice.' *The Washington Post* thought the short running time was long enough – '*Jonah Hex* may not be the longest 81 minutes you ever spend, but it might well be the most tedious.' And the *Boston Herald* compared it unfavourably with an earlier film Michael had been in – 'It's the latest in a long, stinking line of graphic novels adapted to the screen in the wake of the huge, surprise success of Zack Snyder's far superior 2006 effort *300*.'

The movie fared no better in Britain. 'Almost everything is wrong with it,' said the *Daily Mail*. 'Every character is a stereotype, from the macho, scarred bounty hunter who's lost his family and now goes round killin' people to a couple of cackling villains (John Malkovich and Michael Fassbender).' The *Guardian* dismissed it as 'simply wretched, borderline-nonsensical comic-book fantasy'. To the *Observer* it was 'a loud, coarse, overblown adaptation of a comic book, a choppy, sub-Leone affair in which the longest sustained sequence is the rolling of the final credits'.

No one, it seemed, was holding back on their attacks. The *Daily Mirror* highlighted its box-office failure: 'Having already bombed big-time in the US, our search for the biggest turkey of 2010 ends right here.' 'It's a loud and subtle-as-a-sledgehammer assault on the senses, though, at 81 minutes, mercifully short,' said the *Daily Telegraph*. And *Empire* magazine called it, 'an object lesson in how not to adapt a comic book. A crushing disappointment'. Ouch.

Michael had taken time out during the filming of *Jonah Hex* to attend the Cannes Film Festival in May. This event was doubly exciting for him because two of his movies were being presented there for competition – *Fish Tank* and *Inglourious Basterds*. Michael took his parents with him and his father was intrigued to hear his son talking German in the film. 'It's funny to see and hear Michael speaking German with the English accent,' Josef told Killarney newspaper, the *Kingdom*.

Like his son, Josef found Quentin Tarantino to be a fascinating man. 'It was so funny. We were sitting in Cannes, in the hotel lobby having a drink, and Quentin Tarantino come over and says, "Do you mind if I sit here?"' he recalled. 'I said to myself, "Jesus, Mary and Joseph, Tarantino asked if he can sit with us!" But he is a very interesting man. The knowledge the man has – like a computer – and any film you mention he has seen it. What impressed me was his knowledge of Germany. Things that only Germans would know, he knows. He's a man who does his homework well.'

Josef also remarked on his son's choice of roles and his good fortune in having worked with such top film-makers. 'He likes to do different things, to be on the edge, I think. He has been very lucky to work with creative directors. Andrea, I know, likes plays with characters and things like that. Steve McQueen is more visual effect. Then he was with Tom Hanks in *Band of Brothers*. He picked some good ones.'

Both films were short-listed for the main award, the prestigious Palme d'Or, but the prize eventually went to *The White Ribbon*, a film shot in black and white about unexplained violent events in a remote German village in 1913. But *Fish Tank* was a joint winner of the Prix du Jury award, which Andrea had won in 2006 for *Red Road*, and Christoph Waltz won Best Actor for *Inglourious Basterds* for Landa – the role that Michael had wanted!

Quentin was asked by the world's press why his movie's title had such an unusual spelling but he refused to explain. 'Here's the thing. It's not a typo,' he said. 'I'm never going to explain it. When I do an artistic flourish like that, to describe it would be to invalidate the whole process.'

On its commercial release *Inglourious Basterds* received mixed reviews. The *New York Times* called it, 'Simply another testament to his movie love. The problem is that by making the star attraction of his latest film a most delightful Nazi, one whose smooth talk is as lovingly presented as his murderous violence, Mr Tarantino has polluted that love.' The *Los Angeles Times* felt it over-long and rambling – 'A film that loses its way in the thickets of alternative history and manages to be violent without the start-to-finish energy that violence on screen usually guarantees.'

There was a similar view in Britain from the *Daily Telegraph* – 'Tension is evoked, but never mounts. Intrigue is created but never sustained.' The *Daily Mail* agreed but with a more critical edge – 'His warfest is a gore-fest. Yes, it shows off his strengths – clever, suspense-filled dialogue and directorial flair. But it also shows off his weaknesses – long-windedness, a juvenile desire to shock, and unappetising elements of sadism, racism and transatlantic triumphalism.' The British tabloid press proved more receptive. The *People* described it as 'thoroughly enjoyable and a real return to form for Tarantino' and the *Sunday Mirror* hailed it as 'a bloody, all-guns-blazing romp'.

Rolling Stone magazine, while acknowledging that the movie would be divisive, found it ultimately irresistible – 'Will *Basterds* polarise audiences? That's a given. But for anyone professing true movie love, there's no resisting it.'

By this stage of his career, Michael had managed to leave far behind his initial image as 'the man from the Guinness commercial' in Ireland. Now he was invited to hold an acting master class at the Galway Film Fleadh in June, which took place on 11 July. As part of the Fleadh's tribute to him, *Hunger* was screened there. A couple of days later he flew out to Italy to enjoy the revels of the Ischia Global Film & Music Festival before attending Comic Con 2009 in San Diego, California.

If the critics had had their doubts about *Inglourious Basterds*, there was nothing equivocal about their reception of *Fish Tank* when it opened in September. It won rave reviews. 'A neo-kitchen sink drama, *Fish Tank* immediately ranks her [Andrea Arnold] among the greats of social realism, right up there with Tony Richardson, Ken Loach and perhaps even John Osborne,' said the *Daily Mirror*, which called it 'the best British film of the year'. The *Daily Telegraph*, too, was full of praise – 'Well observed and certainly qualifies as one of the most distinctive British releases of 2009.' And *Empire* magazine said it was, 'a vivid portrayal of life at society's margins with a compelling turn from newcomer Jarvis'.

In America the *Chicago Sun-Times* also compared Andrea with Ken Loach, saying, 'Arnold, who won an Oscar for her shattering short film *Wasp*, also about a neglectful alcoholic mother, deserves comparison with a British master director like Ken Loach.' And the *Los Angeles Times* said, 'The brilliant power of the film comes from the gritty reality Arnold creates.'

Andrea had triumphed in her casting. 'The electrifying Fassbender, so good in *Hunger* and *Inglourious Basterds*, nails every nuance in a complex role. His scenes with Jarvis have a hypnotic sexual energy. And while you're remembering new high-impact names, add Arnold. In only her second film, after 2006's *Red Road*, she keeps the screen filled to bursting with the beauty and raw terror of life,' praised *Rolling Stone*. And the Australian film magazine, *Film Ink* agreed – '*Fish Tank* is well shot and uniformly well acted, but especially so by Katie Jarvis and Michael Fassbender.'

Having worked back to back on a string of movies, Michael could now finally afford to take time off to relax, confident that he had established himself as an actor. Financially comfortable enough not to need to rush into any job offered to him, he did little for the rest of the year. His next movie was to take him back to Ireland, where he would be beaten up by a woman.

CHAPTER TEN

LICENSED
TO THRILL?

D irector Steven Soderbergh had been responsible for such cinematic hits as *Ocean's Eleven* and its sequels *Twelve* and *Thirteen*, along with the powerful Oscar-winning drug movie *Traffic* and the acclaimed legal drama *Erin Brockovich*. He had seen Michael in *Hunger* and *Inglourious Basterds* and been impressed. 'My reaction was, "This guy's a movie star." It was blatantly obvious to me,' he recalled. Soderbergh now approached Michael for a brief but scene-stealing role in his new thriller, *Haywire*.

The story centred on Mallory Kane, a highly trained freelance covert operative, hired out by her handler (Ewan McGregor) for hazardous secret missions by the US Government. During an assignment in Dublin with an

Irish assassin, she is betrayed by her employers and pursued across the city by the local police and ruthless hitmen under the command of the CIA official who hired her (Michael Douglas). Realising she can trust no one, she heads back home to hide out at the house of her father (Bill Paxton). As her enemies close in, she is determined to discover the truth and the part played by a shadowy Spanish official (Antonio Banderas).

Spielberg had cast mixed-martial-arts supremo Gina Carano as Kane and turned to Michael to play the cool and clinical killer, Paul, a former MI6 operative now doing freelance work. Michael described him as 'highly paranoid and self-serving. I don't think there's much about him that is compassionate towards anyone or anything. He has a mercenary type of personality.'

Michael had not heard of Gina when Steven told him about her over the phone and asked Michael if he minded being beaten up by a woman! Michael said he didn't mind and then started to check out some of her fights on YouTube. 'I thought, "This looks like fun!"' he recalled. Filming began at the start of February 2010. The scene with Gina was set in a Dublin hotel room, where they are pretending to be husband and wife while on a mission. Gina is suspicious of Paul, who she doesn't know, but is taken aback when he suddenly attacks her in the room. The impressive but brutal fight sequence involves them throwing each other around and picking up whatever comes to hand to hurt each other with.

The movie's stunt team were the same ones that Michael had worked with on *300* so he felt comfortable with them. They, in turn, knew his capabilities so he and Gina were allowed to do the whole fight sequence themselves. 'I had a lot of fun doing that. We did all of that ourselves, which actors get very proud about!' Michael told *Total Film* magazine. 'I enjoy doing physical stuff. Fight scenes are fun but someone like Gina can literally do it for real. I'm good at pretending!'

It took a lot of effort, careful choreography and precise timing by both of them to make it look so realistic. 'It looks really violent but the classic thing when you're doing fight sequences is that the person who's getting thrown is doing the leading and the person who's grabbing someone's hair, they're doing the following. So you just try and make it look frenetic and violent, when actually you're just looking out for each other and making sure nobody gets hurt.

'Because you've got to do it over two days and you've got to keep repeating it, there's no point getting all gung-ho and losing control. I don't like doing fight sequences with people who lose control. It's not a comfortable place to be and that's when people get hurt.'

But neither of them escaped completely unscathed. When Gina had to smash a vase against his head, Michael was told to turn his head as the specially constructed vase hit him. But instead he looked at it and took the full force in his face. 'Everything went bright for a few seconds and, of course, that's the take they used!' he laughed later. This incident was balanced out by Gina breaking her finger on Michael's shoulder! In another fight scene with Ewan McGregor, McGregor accidentally kicked Gina in the head. But she wasn't bothered and asked him if *he* was all right.

Michael joked that in real life Gina 'would beat the shit out of me. The fact that Gina is a very physical person and she's got great command over her body, it made her the perfect partner – because then you can really push things and know that she's capable. She was actually saying, "Drive me into the television. But really hard." I was like, "You know, we're acting here, Gina, we're not in the ring. Let's establish that before it's your turn to start hitting me!"'

After the adrenalin of the fight scene had worn off, Michael admitted that he was physically sick. 'We filmed that whole fight over two days and at the end of the second day I just remember I came back to my hotel room and I puked up,' he said. 'It's amazing when your body's running on adrenaline and then you reach the finish line it just goes, "fuck it!"'

Michael got on well with Gina. 'I really liked her a lot. She's brave as an actress as well,' he told *In Style* magazine. 'She was ballsy and open to adapting on the spot. Just really game. She's lethal but she's really sweet and quite a shy person actually. So there's a great paradox there, which I guess is really interesting for directors. She's got a vulnerability but also a real steeliness.'

Michael believed that Soderbergh's decision to cast Gina in the lead role, despite her having barely any experience of acting, had been brave and inspirational. 'Steven doesn't really adhere to any set of rules. He's always willing to try things if he has a gut instinct about somebody. He sees something and then runs with it. It's really exciting and inspiring to be around that.'

It was also in Dublin that one evening Steven saw how the actor had acquired his reputation as a party animal. 'He's a blast,' the director told the *Hollywood Reporter*. 'We're out one night and it's 3.30am, and we're in someone's kitchen and Michael is singing. I'm like, '"Dude, I gotta go."' The phrase Michael uses most often is, "So where are we going now?" He's the Duracell movie star!'

Michael also got on well with Ewan McGregor, whom he considered to be down to earth. Like Michael, Ewan is a keen motorcyclist and they spent much of their time talking about bikes.

The ice-cool, debonair yet ruthless Paul brought to mind James Bond. At the time *Haywire* was released Daniel Craig was filming his third 007 movie, *Skyfall*, and it prompted some to wonder whether Michael was aiming to be the next actor to slip into Bond's tuxedo. He found himself being asked this by interviewers on several occasions and, while doing his best to play it cool, he couldn't hide the fact that he fancied the role. 'I think Daniel [Craig] is doing a great job and I don't think too far into the future. It's one step at a time right now,' he told *Total Film*, before adding, 'Of course, every guy knows the feeling of walking round the house singing the song to himself, walking around corners with an imaginary gun. Let's see what happens.'

While back in Ireland Michael was invited onto RTE's top chat programme, *The Late Late Show,* hosted by Ryan Tubridy. When asked whether the fame and accolades that came his way in the wake of *Hunger* had affected him, he laughed and replied, 'Most of the time it's like, "Jesus, I've managed to get away with another one." You're always expecting a fall after stuff like that. But I don't read reviews. Noel Coward said that, if you read the good reviews, you have to read the bad ones. And it becomes a distraction as well.'

At the end of the interview Ryan surprised him by saying that there was a rumour that he could 'hold a tune'. Michael laughed and looked a little embarrassed before Ryan told him to 'get over there with the band' To applause and cheers from the audience, he got up and walked over and launched into a rousing performance of the Beatles hit *Twist and Shout*. The rendition sounded like that of a young John Lennon – more of a dynamic, hoarse yell than singing. It underlined Michael's natural and sometimes subconscious ability for mimicry – echoing Lennon one moment but also adept at Sinatra-like singing. He could also do excellent impersonations of Quentin Tarantino and Christopher Walken.

Back home in Hackney, Michael attended the London Critics Circle Film Awards at the Landmark Hotel on 18 February, where *Fish Tank* won awards for Best British Film, Best British Director, Best Young British Performer for Katie Jarvis and Best British Actor in a Supporting Role for Michael. There was success, too, for *Inglourious Basterds*, with Christoph Waltz named as Best Actor of the Year for his portrayal of Colonel Landa and Quentin Tarantino collecting an Outstanding Achievement award.

A day later Michael and Liam Cunningham went to Ireland's top musical awards ceremony, the Meteor Ireland Music Awards, in Dublin, where they enjoyed live performances from the likes of Florence and the Machine, Pixie Lott, The Script and Westlife.

Michael would miss out on glory at that year's IFTAS in Dublin, where Colin Farrell won Best Actor for his performance in Neil Jordan's *Ondine*, but by then he was already thinking about his next role – Mr Rochester in *Jane Eyre*. Then came a bolt out of the blue. Always cautious about talking about his private life, he was about to have it splashed across the world's newspapers, websites and news bulletins.

CHAPTER ELEVEN

THE ROAD TO ROCHESTER

After less than a year together, Michael had split up with Leasi Andrews in the autumn of 2009. But on 10 March 2010 he was staggered when she sensationally applied for a restraining order against him. Michael refused to comment publicly on the accusations and Josef told the *Irish Sun*, 'Michael is the most gentle man you could ever meet.'

In the meantime, Michael went home to Killarney, where he acted as grand marshal for the St Patrick's Day parade on 17 March. Hiding his personal concerns, he was all smiles as he arrived at a civic reception held by the town council where Major Michael Gleeson presented him with a pen made of Arbutus Killarney wood and a Killarneycrested tie. Later he headed the parade in a horse-drawn carriage, accompanied by Major Gleeson, as his proud parents looked on.

'I'm overwhelmed. It's a great honour to be involved here today,' he said in between signing autographs and posing for photographs with fans. 'It feels quite surreal but it's very pleasant. There's a general feeling of support, of encouragement and lots of love – all the happy faces I see when I walk the streets of Killarney.' Grinning broadly and laughing, he threw himself boisterously into some traditional dancing in the streets with the Irwin School of Irish Dancing.

The annual parade had been organised for many years by Councillor Michael Courtney, the father of Donie Courtney whose acting classes had first inspired Michael back in his schooldays. Sadly, Courtney senior had died unexpectedly earlier in the year, shortly before he was due to take up the post of the town's mayor, so this year's parade was held in his memory. More than 60 groups and floats and 6 bands participated in the parade and afterwards Mr Courtney's councillor son, Hugh, thanked everyone for making it such a success.

'I would like to thank Michael for travelling back from his busy filming schedule for the parade that honoured the memory of my father,' he said. 'Michael has for a long time been a friend of the Courtney family, from the days he and I spent together in the Sem, right through to his acting connections with my brother, Donie. Michael has been and I hope will continue to be a wonderful ambassador for Killarney and we wish him continued success in his acting career.'

The following day Michael went back to his two former schools. First he visited Fossa National School where the young children screamed, cheered and waved homemade banners as he arrived. There to meet him were principal Kieran Coffey and two of his former teachers, Linda O'Donoghue and Angela Lynch, who had fond memories of him when they taught him in the late 1980s.

Michael said he had many happy memories of the years he spent in Fossa and made a nostalgic visit to his old classroom, where he found his former desk. He happily posed for photographs with the staff and signed many autographs for the star-struck pupils who took part in a question-and-answer session with him. One particular question amused teachers and movie star alike when a young child asked him what it was like to meet Ryan Tubridy on *The Late Late Show*. Michael was also entertained by the pupils singing a medley of songs from classic movies and he joined in enthusiastically with the singing.

After spending well over an hour at Fossa, the next stop was St Brendan's College, where he had attended secondary school in the 1990s. He was introduced to a packed canteen by popular English teacher Seamus Grealy, and Michael chatted with the students before picking up a guitar and playing a few songs.

Four days later he was in Derbyshire to begin filming *Jane Eyre*. Set in the Peak District in the 19th century, Charlotte Bronte's classic novel tells the story of Jane, who is treated cruelly as a child by her aunt and is sent to a brutal boarding school. After a couple of years as a teacher she advertises her services as a governess, and receives one reply. It is from Alice Fairfax, the housekeeper at Thornfield Hall, a remote house in the Yorkshire Peak District. Here she teaches a young French girl named Adele and finds a friend in the kindly Miss Fairfax. Jane settles comfortably into her role. One day while she is out walking, a horse slips and throws its rider to the ground. She helps the man back on and later, back at the house, discovers that he is Edward Rochester, master of Thornfield Hall. He teases her, asking whether she had bewitched his horse to make him fall, and the two strike up an intriguing and flirtatious relationship. Adele, it transpires, was left in Rochester's care when her mother died.

Meanwhile, odd things are happening in the house. A mysterious fire breaks out and Jane hears a strange laugh that nobody else admits to hearing. Jane is heartbroken over Rochester's impending marriage to Blanche Ingram. But on a summer's evening he suddenly proposes to Jane and she accepts. But she is frightened one night when a savage-looking woman enters her bedroom and rips her wedding veil in two. Rochester attributes the incident to drunkenness on the part of one of his servants, Grace

Poole, whom he also blamed for the fire. But if that were so, why does he continue to employ her?

Rochester eventually leads Jane to the altar but it is dramatically declared that he cannot marry because he is still married. Rochester admits this to Jane but explains that his father had tricked him into the marriage for her money. After the ceremony, he had discovered that his bride was rapidly descending into madness and he eventually locked her away in Thornfield, hiring Grace Poole as a nurse to look after her. But whenever Grace has too much to drink, his wife escapes and causes the strange happenings at Thornfield. He begs her forgiveness and asks her to go with him to the south of France but Jane runs away.

Years later she returns after hearing that Rochester's wife had set the house on fire and committed suicide by jumping from the roof. In his attempt to rescue her from the fire, he had lost a hand and his eyesight. Jane expresses her love for him and says she will never leave him again.

Michael admitted to feeling nervous about taking on such a well-known role but his mother and sister were such big fans of the Bronte sisters that he wanted to see what they thought of him as Rochester. 'For sure, there's a fear element involved,' he told *GQ* magazine. 'The novel alone is an amazing piece of work that you want to do justice to. I like that fear with me when I enter most jobs. If I don't have that fear, I'm complacent, I'm in a comfort zone, so I want to be there. I want to continue learning as much as I can. Fear is a healthy thing – it keeps you disciplined. You have to make sure you've done your homework.'

When Michael learned that the film was to be directed by Cary Fukunaga he became very excited. Michael had loved the American director's acclaimed film *Sin Nombre*, a Spanish-language movie about Mexican gang members trying to escape to the United States. '*Sin Nombre* was such a good film, such a beautiful story and so beautifully told. I was like, "This is going to be interesting – an American director coming over and doing his take on this, the classic British piece,"' he recalled.

As with *Fish Tank*, Michael felt that the characters in *Jane Eyre* had depth and were multi-faceted, behaving unpredictably in various circumstances. 'I like that the characters are ugly and they're beautiful and they're cruel and they're nurturing. There's so much complexity to them, they're so well written, and I find that interesting. There's an ambiguity within them. You're wondering where things will lead. Are they going to nourish each other or rip each other apart? That's why people keep coming back to these characters, because they are so well thought out – as opposed to formulaic stories where, after the first ten minutes, you know where the arc of a character is going to go. This is ever changing, keeping the audience on their toes. And that's what really attracted me to it, to the performance.'

Alison Owen, who produced *Jane Eyre*, said that Cary

Fukunaga only ever wanted Michael for the part of Rochester. And she seemed just as enamoured with him – if not more so – than the director. 'He's dream casting,' she said. 'He has a natural air of mystery, which is perfect for the role of Rochester. A number of *Jane Eyre* films have failed because Rochester wasn't strong enough. And Michael is obviously very good looking and sexy, which helps.'

Despite the fact that Rochester had been portrayed in many film and television adaptations before, Michael found his own insights into how to bring something new to the role. 'The first thing that struck me and I thought was quite interesting about Rochester is that he seems to be sort of bi-polar,' he told the *Hollywood Reporter*. 'His emotions are very skittish and can go from high to low very quickly.

'He is like a Byronic hero. He's cruel, he's arrogant, he's intelligent, he's sort of without a social standing so even though he is of the aristocracy he doesn't really like that crowd. He doesn't see the barriers between the social classes as it were, so he's quite a fair person, and in some respect I like that.'

Michael also had the feeling that Rochester had been to some very decadent places in his life and that his guilt and bitterness and sense of a lost youth have remained with him and can sometimes be seen in flashes. It's through Jane that he becomes healed, so he wanted to show a sick person in some respect and, by the end, he's found a peace and reconciliation.

Perhaps surprisingly, Fukunaga knew he had found his Rochester after seeing Michael in a very different role – as Bobby Sands in *Hunger*. 'I hadn't seen that sort of fierceness in an actor in a long time,' he explained. 'There was an intelligence, an intensity and a masculinity that is very difficult to find in a leading man. Michael can be tortured and still be intelligent and communicate through his eyes and his emotions all the stress of the life Rochester's lived but also still have that sense of humour, which is key to their attraction to each other.'

In the title role was 20-year-old Australian actress Mia Wasikowska, who had starred in Tim Burton's *Alice in Wonderland*. Michael had not expected her to be quite as good as she was. After he began working with her, he described Mia as being 'the future of acting' and 'really something special'.

Michael was delighted when Dame Judi Dench was cast as the housekeeper, Mrs Fairfax. Like many others before and since, he was bowled over by her professionalism, kindness and mischievousness. 'I feel blessed every day being able to talk to her,' he said during a break in filming. 'Whatever gold dust is on her, I hope it will fall onto my shoulders! It's a real privilege to be able to work with her.'

As for Fukunaga, Michael found the director to be 'intelligent' and 'a perfectionist who tries to get the best out of everything – every shot, every moment, every beat.' He also believed Cary had an advantage as an American who hadn't grown up with the book. It meant that he wasn't so reverent and brought a fresh eye to the story and had the confidence to make bold decisions. 'He's a real academic, he does his research and he knows how to frame a shot so beautifully.'

There was much humour during filming when Michael had to ride a rather flatulent horse named Prince. 'We had a pretty interesting bond!' he joked later. 'Every time I got on him some strange stuff was happening "downstairs" so we'd have to get the horse handler and he would get on Prince and take him for a trot down the road and the horse would come back more settled.'

But the spring weather proved to be rather wet, which caused some delays and that, combined with some niggling production problems, was making Cary feel a bit down. Michael lifted spirits his spirits when he invited him, Mia and producer Alison Owen for dinner, when he cooked and served a splendid dish of his father's speciality – rack of lamb. 'We all just sat around and enjoyed one of the small, perfect things in life – a good meal,' said Cary. 'And I remembered exactly why you make movies. It's not just about the project but about the process, and I think one thing that makes Michael special is his ability to stop and pause for a second.'

Mia also found him great fun to work with. 'We were perfectly matched in that we were able to counter the intensity of our scenes together with a lot of goofing around,' she said. 'Michael's just so incredible. He's so charismatic himself. We got on so well and we were able to have a lot of fun and then channel that fun into the intensity of the material.'

Even during romantic scenes the pair got the giggles. A moment of particular sexual tension between them, when Rochester and Jane nearly kiss, was almost ruined when Mia felt the urge to laugh. It was the last scene they had to film and by that stage everyone was tired and pleased to be near the end so they could shake off their characters and rest. Just like the last day of school term, the anticipation and excitement expressed itself in high jinks, silliness and giggles. 'I was off my rocker that day and I remember trying to reel it in to have the seriousness to do this scene,' Mia told *Total Film*.

Imogen Poots, with whom Michael had worked with on *Centurion*, played socialite Blanche Ingram whom Mr Rochester courts in order to make Jane jealous. The role required her and Michael to perform operetta duets and both actors, at times, found it hard to keep a straight face. They later joked that they would always have a duet up their sleeves should it ever come in useful in future.

In an interview with *Glamour* magazine, in which Michael discussed playing the romantic leading man, he was asked what the most romantic thing he had ever done for a woman was. Never one to talk much about such things, he replied, 'I don't know. I always think surprise holidays are pretty good. Just packing a bag and going to the airport. Give them some idea of what to pack but not too much idea. That's good fun.'

His interviewer also posed another question that showed an insight into his interests. When asked which period in history he would most like to live in and why, he replied, 'I'd like to be a musician in the 1960s because it seemed like a lot of fun and there was a lot of shared creative talent. The fact that you could walk into a room and maybe John Lennon was sitting there and Bob Marley and Mick Jagger, just jamming. Or I would like to be a Formula 1 driver in the late 1970s, early 1980s. That would be kind of cool.'

Even better was the news that came in early April, a few weeks into filming. Leasi Andrews had asked a Los Angeles Superior Court judge to dismiss her petition and claims.

CHAPTER TWELVE

SPANKING
KEIRA

Earlier in the year Michael had been contacted by the controversial director of *Crash*, *eXistenZ* and *Eastern Promises*, David Cronenberg. Over lunch at his home in Toronto, he discussed his new film and the role he had in mind for Michael, who was immediately intrigued. The movie, which centred on the birth of psychoanalysis, was to be scripted by Christopher Hampton from his play *The Talking Cure*, itself an adaptation from the book *A Most Dangerous Method* by John Kerr.

The story revolved around the friendship and rivalry of psychoanalysis' two foremost practitioners, Sigmund Freud and Carl Jung. In the beginning Jung, the younger of the two, idolises Freud and the pioneering work he has done in this new field. He is thrilled to meet him and even withstands his patronising air but, as his confidence grows and his own work develops, Jung begins to feel that his experiments in dream analysis are a step up from Freud's obsession with sex. The two men cannot agree, yet ironically it is Jung who is experiencing for real the type of behaviour that Freud is known to analyse.

When an 18-year-old Russian girl, Sabina Spielrein, is admitted with severe hysteria to the Swiss hospital where Jung works, he takes a keen interest in her. She tells him that she is 'vile and filthy and corrupt' before finally confessing that she found the spanking that her father gave her as a child to be thrilling, and that she longs to be spanked again. At first Jung is very professional and proper in his approach to treating her, using Freud's analytical methods, but the sexual tension between them yawns open after a conversation Jung has with fellow psychiatrist Otto Gross, who is joyously amoral and whose motto is 'Never repress anything'. Jung – growing increasingly distant from his pregnant wife – begins a sado-masochistic affair with Sabina and, in so doing, puts even more strain on his relationship with a disapproving Freud.

With filming on *Jane Eyre* wrapped by mid-May, Michael focused on reading the script for *A Dangerous Method*. He had been offered the role of Jung, which he had accepted, alongside Viggo Mortensen as Freud and Keira Knightley as Sabina. As was his practice, Michael read the script over and over again and continued to do so throughout filming, which began in mid-June.

The film has become particularly known for the scene in which Jung spanks Sabina. It was something that both actors were worried about and Keira had initially turned down the role because of it. But in their phone call Cronenberg was so keen to keep her on board that he offered to cut the scene. Keira then had second thoughts because she realised how important it was to the piece and she agreed to do it. 'He [Cronenberg] said he didn't want the scenes to be sexy or voyeuristic. He wanted them to be clinical and a complete exploration of what she was feeling,' said Keira. 'So we kind of came to an agreement with Michael as well – because he had questions about the scene. I wanted it to be as shocking as possible without going over the top.'

But Michael was relieved to find that, despite such deep and dark human yearnings and complex psychoanalytical issues, there was also humour to be found in the script. 'I found the script funny,' he told the Scottish TV channel STV. 'When I was rehearsing with Viggo, I said, "This is funny, right?" and so we did explore that side of it as well as the highbrow stuff, the world of academia and psychoanalysis, to find those moments of humour. I think the idea that makes Jung really interesting for me was that he said, "How can I diagnose the patient if I don't experience what the patient is experiencing?" This encompasses the passion that he had.'

The bond between Jung and Sabina becomes very strong after he helps to release her inner demons. 'Before, she found her needs dirty or something she needed to hide. It wasn't socially acceptable for a woman to be feeling those things,' explained Michael. 'That she was such an intelligent person intrigued him even more. He also feels he's really fulfilling her desires by spanking her. I think he's turned on by her getting turned on.

'She arrives as this hysteric and Jung is very much the doctor who's in control. By the end of the film, though, when he has somewhat unravelled, the roles have sort of reversed. She's become an analyst in her own right, which is such a cool thing, that someone can come in as a patient and leave as a doctor.'

When it came to filming the spanking scene, both Michael and Keira had a couple of vodka shots to steady their nerves. With the camera placed in front of them, Michael actually hit a cushion to one side of Keira as he stood behind her. He was nervous about getting his aim right. 'It's always embarrassing and awkward when you do stuff like that. You try to keep the atmosphere light,' he recalled. 'I didn't want to actually hit her so I was concentrating on hitting the mark and not her.'

Accidentally being hit was also on Keira's mind. 'We were both very nervous about those scenes,' she said. 'When we shot them I said to Michael, "If you touch me, I'm going to kill you." He said, "Keira, you're tied to the bed at the moment. I don't think you're in any position to say that!"'

Michael was full of praise for Keira for being brave and throwing herself into it. 'She took on board the physicality and how it manifests itself and all credit to her because she was so brave and ready and prepared. We were four days ahead after week one because David had put aside a section of time for those tricky scenes. But she was a real pleasure to work with – she was an absolute pro.'

After they had successfully finished the spanking scene the pair of them celebrated with a couple of glasses of champagne. 'You can count on Michael to buy a bottle of champagne when one is required,' said Keira. 'The vodka and champagne is a good combination.' As a parting gift she gave Michael a spanking paddle on which she had written, 'I wouldn't have been spanked by anyone but you. Lots of love, Keira.'

Viggo Mortensen was taken aback when he first started filming his scenes with Michael. As he recalled on *The Late Show With David Letterman*, 'Michael is a very physical guy and he wanted to be kind of leaping at me in our scenes. So he did this thing before every shot where he would hop on one foot, like he had a skipping rope. And he wanted this lean angry look – an intense stare – so he would cover one eye with his hand while he was hopping. Keira was fine with it and would just look away but I didn't know what to make of it. He would take his hand away from his eye at the last minute before we did a scene and he would stare at me almost cross-eyed.

'There was one scene where we were on a sailing boat – the one time I was really worried. I'm sitting down and he was standing, steering and working the sail, and he starts jumping again. And I'm thinking, "He's going to put a hole right in the bottom of the boat." It was really scary.'

The film's producer, Jeremy Thomas, was surprised to see Michael reading the script over and over again during filming, something he had never seen an actor do before. Michael described the process as being one of his 'secret weapons' when it came to acting. It enabled him to find new nuances to plot and character and helped him to relax and be more comfortable with the words when it came to filming.

Michael also turned to his sister Catherine – now a neuropsychologist specialising in ADHD (Attention Deficit Hyperactivity Disorder) in children at UC Davis – to understand more about psychology. Catherine was a fan of Jung and loved the idea that her brother was portraying him. 'Even though my sister is scientific, she is of that belief that there are a lot of unanswered things out there that science hasn't yet been able to explain, or perhaps never will,' said Michael, 'so I think she likes that mystic element to Jung.'

He also turned to YouTube again to watch footage of Jung as an older man. But it was when Michael put on the spectacles and costume of his character – the waistcoat, moustache, stiff collar, side parting – that he really felt the part. 'There was a real elegance about the time and it always helps when you put on a costume,' he explained. 'You do all your homework at home and then slowly you put on the shoes that the character wears, and all the intricate little things, like a pocket watch. It helps to give you that certain way of sort of holding yourself, and I love all that.

'Jung and Freud were pioneers. They were trying to understand how we function and what separates us from animals, and with certain things ask, "Are we that far apart from animals?" Freud would say that we do respond because of our physicality and our relationship to our physicality.

'These were the first guys talking about penises and vaginas and the anus and the mouth, about sexuality and our primal urges, and how these things will affect us in our adult lives and how we always carry that around with us and how they are there and should be recognised and explored, otherwise they can run amok – otherwise madness can ensue and violence and all sorts of primal things.'

Michael and Viggo also got the chance to look at the written correspondence between the two men and they were struck by how beautiful the handwriting was. It was apparent that the art of letter writing was a very important weapon and tool in those days. The power of the language they used and the eloquent way it was expressed would be a vital way of putting an argument across and anyone in the academic field lacking in this skill would be at a serious disadvantage.

Shooting took place in Cologne, the Bodensee (Lake Constance) and Vienna – where Freud had lived for many years – across eight weeks. The director, so provocative in his films, was bemused by Michael's seemingly permanent upbeat and happy nature. 'He's so perky, it drives you crazy,' he said. 'One day I found him out in the sun in his costume and make-up, with this big smile. I said, "Michael, why are you smiling like that?" He said, "I don't know... life." I said, "It's so irritating that you're happy all the time."'

For Michael, working with Cronenberg proved to be a memorable and fascinating experience. 'He's a director who is interested in scratching [below] the surface,' he told *Total Film*. 'We live in this civilised society where we're supposed to behave in certain ways and there's an etiquette at play. What happens when you peel back the covers and look underneath and how do we actually deal with each other in practical terms as opposed to theoretically? So when there's a curiosity in a director like that, you know it's going to be interesting, that the characters are going to be more complex and it's going to be a really intelligent introspection.'

Working on the film and researching Jung, Freud and the world of psychoanalysis did make Michael think about what makes people, happy, sad or just content with their lives. 'If you look at our society now it's very much obsessed with the "I'" – how can I become more successful? How can I become more charming? How do I get ahead in life? I think it's gone to the extreme and I think we need to think more about what we can do collectively and focus on those around us more. And I think happiness can lie there as much as it can through self-introspection.'

On the publicity trail for *A Dangerous Method*, Keira became convinced that the English were obsessed with spanking. 'People liked the spanking an awful lot,' she told *Interview* magazine. 'But it's weird. When we were in Venice, I didn't get asked about it once in however many days we were there. And then in Toronto I got asked about it a little bit more. But in England, it was pretty much the only thing I got asked about.'

In between his hectic film schedule Michael found time to voice the main character of Logan in the third video game in the *Fable* series of role-playing adventures in which the player/character struggles to overthrow the King of Albion by forming alliances and building support for a revolution. *Fable III* was set 50 years on from the previous instalment, with the monarch's son, Logan, now ruling the Kingdom of Albion. The game included a star cast of voice talents including Ben Kingsley, Stephen Fry, Simon Pegg, Zoe Wanamaker and John Cleese. It was released on 29 October 2010.

In the mean time Michael, who had made a name for himself from a string of interesting independent films that had won him acclaim and awards, was now being offered big studio pictures. And the one he settled on was to reach a huge worldwide audience and fully establish him as a star.

CHAPTER THIRTEEN

AN X-CELLENT
MOVE

Although Michael was more of a *Beano* and *Dandy* reader as a boy than a fan of superhero comics, he did think he was Superman and had fantasised over Wonder Woman, so maybe his next choice wasn't so unusual. As worldwide movie franchises went they didn't come much bigger than this. The four previous *X-Men* movies – *X-Men*, *X-2*, *X-Men: The Last Stand* and *X-Men Origins: Wolverine* – had been hugely successful and he had enjoyed watching them.

The stories were set in a world of ordinary humans and mutants with strong and strange special powers, which are feared by the rest of the citizens. When a US senator hounds the mutants and wants them to register with the government in order to protect others, it causes friction and resentment. Several mutants find solace at Professor Charles Xavier's school, which teaches them how to harness their special powers. And so we have the likes of Jean Grey, who has telekinetic and telepathic skills, Storm, who can manipulate weather disturbances, Cyclops, whose eyes release energy blasts, and Wolverine, who has healing powers. But danger looms when fellow mutant Magneto, who can control magnetic fields that manipulate metal, concocts a plan to turn the world's leaders into mutants at a special UN gathering. Xavier forms a crack team of mutants called The X-Men to fight Magneto and his fellow rebels.

Michael liked that the stories were grounded on such enduring social and psychological issues as ostracism, conflict, fear and resentment. He was impressed by the script for the new movie, *X-Men: First Class*, which was a prequel explaining how Magneto and Xavier first met and became friends before falling out. He immersed himself in reading *X-Men* comic-book stories and thought that there was more depth and characterisation to them than many others of the genre.

He was also a fan of the movie's British director Matthew Vaughn, who had previously directed the superhero comedy *Kick-Ass*. He was also aware of the benefits of a blockbuster movie reaching a wide audience, raising his profile and giving him more control over his career. 'I've been around for a while and I've had to graft to get to the position I'm in, and I wouldn't change a bit of that. If it's a success, it allots me more power, which allows me to control my own career more,' he said.

The story for *X-Men: First Class* was described by Vaughn as '*X–Men* meets the Cuban missile crisis meets James Bond.' It begins at a German concentration camp in Poland during World War II when young Erik Lensherr is separated from his parents by Nazi guards. In his frustration and anger he bends a metal gate without touching it, using magnetic power. Nazi scientist Sebastian Shaw, who has observed this through a window, calls Erik up to see him. Placing a metal coin on a desk, he orders him to use his power to move it. When Erik cannot, Shaw shoots and kills his mother in front of him. His rage sends his power out of control, wrecking the room and killing two guards. A delighted Shaw is determined to harness the boy's power.

The story then jumps to 1962 when Erik is still trying to track down Shaw to get his revenge. When a banker refuses to help, Erik shows just how ruthless he has become, by using his mind's power to rip a metal filling from the terrified man's mouth. It gets him talking and Erik manages to trace a bar of gold to Shaw's address in Argentina. Meanwhile, Shaw and a bunch of mutants with trained super powers are planning to start a world war. CIA agent Moira MacTaggart seeks the help of Oxford University graduate Charles Xavier, who is publishing his thesis on mutation.

The telepathic and telekinetic Xavier uses his power to discover that Shaw – who is a mutant himself – wants to manipulate the Cuban missile crisis to start a nuclear war between the US and Russia in order to wipe out all normal humans. Xavier then starts to train a team of mutants at his mansion home, turning them into an elite fighting force to stop them. In one spectacular scene, Erik raises a nuclear submarine out of the sea using his magnetic mind control.

Towards the end of the movie, an increasingly dangerous Erik admits that he agrees with Shaw that the only way for mutants to live a hassle-free life is to destroy humans. From now on he will be known as Magneto. We then see him wearing a cool-looking helmet to underline his new alter ego, which sets things up nicely for the next movie in the series or, as Michael mischievously put it, 'I've got the purple helmet and I'm ready for action.'

Michael was cast as Lensherr/Magneto in the role previously played by Sir Ian McKellen, while James McAvoy, with whom Michael had worked on *Band of Brothers* and who had gone on to star in *Atonement* and *The Last King of Scotland*, took Patrick Stewart's place as a young Xavier. Michael initially looked to base his portrayal on McKellen as a younger man but Vaughn wasn't keen on the idea so he delved into the comic books and found a wealth of material to draw on. 'Erik speaks German, goes to a concentration camp in Poland, ends up in Eastern Europe and then goes off to Israel. There's so much there and I tried to approach it freshly from the source material,' he explained. 'I wanted to show there is a massive well of history in this character. He is a very damaged individual.'

Michael was much more intrigued by this aspect of Erik than he was by his super power and he liked the idea of the blurring of the line between villain and hero. 'That's way more interesting than just some guy, some baddie, who breezes though an action film. It adds a whole new dimension to the idea of a villain,' he said. And he found that he shared some of Erik's views on society and was aware of the resonance that the film's message had today.

'It was very clear to me what Magneto's opinions were in terms of how much humanity can be trusted,' he said. 'And listen, I love people, I believe we all need each other, that's the essential thing for me in life. In the world it gets lost nowadays when people are all about the "I" – how can I become successful? How can I get ahead? We're obsessed about the individual as opposed to working together. And it does seem to be a human trait that, when we see something we're afraid of, we try to destroy it rather than understand it.'

Michael was impressed by the sophistication of the X-Men comic-book stories. 'You can have a fantastical world around it but at the core there's the really interesting topic of racism and prejudice and people feeling like outsiders,' he told the *Sunday Times*. 'You've got the civil-rights movement at the time we set this film in. You've got all these elements of racism and prejudice and fear of the unknown, and the fear of something within and how society reacts to those things.'

Alongside Michael in the cast were Nicholas Hoult as Beast, Jennifer Lawrence as Raven, January Jones as Emma Frost, Jason Flemyng as the demonic Azazel, Lucas Till as Havoc and Zoë Kravitz as Wings. Most of them, including Michael, were signed up for two further *X-Men* films.

Michael enjoyed the experience of working with Matthew Vaughn. 'He's great because he makes films as a fan,' he told *Total Film*. 'There's something like a nine-year-old boy in him when he's making a film. He allows the characters to drive the plot and the plot to drive the action, as opposed to action driving the film and threading in some sort of a plot.'

Michael tried to take the edge off his Irish accent but Matthew told him not to, explaining that the reason that Sean Connery was the best James Bond was that he had a quirk to his accent and it wasn't straight English. 'I was like, "Great! I can make Magneto Irish!"' Michael joked with the *Irish Voice*. 'He was in hiding in Cork or Kerry for a couple of years after the war. That's where we sort of went with it.'

The film's scriptwriter, Simon Kinberg, thought Michael perfectly captured the almost dual personality of Eric Lehnsherr and his conflicting emotions. 'Because Michael is such an interesting actor, he'll never be "full-on" anything. He'll have a villainous side and he'll have a sympathetic human side you'll be able to relate to but you'll also be afraid of him.'

Having read all the X-Men stories, Michael thought that the relationship between Magneto and Xavier was fascinating. He likened it to two great political leaders, who are enemies but able to sit down and have lunch together and be very amiable towards each other.

Prior to casting, Michael screentested with James McAvoy and the two found they had a great rapport. As James recalled, 'It was very important that the actors playing Xavier and Magneto, who are at the emotional core of the story, got on together and, when we met up, we hit it off and I think we both thought, "Please, God, let it be us two." We share a similar sense of humour and we knew we could push things a bit and not get too serious. We had a great old time.'

They did that. In fact, some of their high jinks were a cause of concern to the director once filming began at Pinewood Studios. One of their favourite games during breaks was to race to a golf buggy that was used for transporting cast to and fro. Michael usually beat James to it but one day James got there first and took the wheel as Michael jumped in the back. Despite it only going at 12mph, James lost control as they drove into a caravan park and crashed into a Lexus car. James tumbled out and Michael went flying over the back seat, banged his head on the steering wheel and ended up in the driver's seat and so got the blame!

A dazed James, who had flown 10 feet, stood up and looked at Michael in the driving seat, laughing madly. As some of the crew gathered around, shaking their heads, Michael simply ran off. James proved to be unhurt but Michael cut his left shin, which has left him with a permanent scar. 'It's my little memento!' he said, laughing.

There were many times when they joked that playing superheroes and villains seemed an odd thing for grown men to do but, in truth, James greatly admired the way Michael brought gravitas to his role. 'No matter how much at times we were thinking, "This is silly as shit," Michael's got the ability and the presence of mind and the intelligence to be able to elevate it,' he said, 'and that was immediately evident from the first moment we sat down and started talking. I think he's really at home with who he is and that's not something that every actor has. He has self-possession in bucketloads and that lends itself to screen presence. While he's on screen, he is in command. He is him.'

On a more relaxed level, Jason Flemyng, who had starred in *Lock, Stock and Two Smoking Barrels* and *Snatch*, both produced by Matthew Vaughn, invited the cast to his place for dinner. Michael, no mean cook himself, having helped his chef father at the family restaurant, was impressed with the slow-roasted pork belly Jason served up. 'It was excellent,' he recalled. 'I was supposed to reciprocate but never did.'

During the making of the film, Michael began a romance with one of his co-stars, 22-year-old Zoe Kravitz – the daughter of singer and musician Lenny Kravitz and actress Lisa Bonet – who played Angel Salvadore. But, intensely private as ever, he refused to confirm or deny it when asked by reporters. 'My private life is private,' he told the *Guardian*. 'If I do a film, how can I expect the audience to follow me if they're thinking, "He goes out with this person" and, "He has this for breakfast"? It's a disadvantage.'

On the subject of increased celebrity and public recognition in the streets following *X-Men* exposure, he was typically level headed. 'I don't think about it too much. I still go about doing my everyday things like I did ten years ago. I don't want to change that. I'm in a privileged position.'

When a reporter from the *Irish Examiner* asked him how difficult it was to go from a small-budget art-house movie like *Hunger* to the blockbuster of *X-Men*, he referred back to his schooldays at St Brendan's. 'It's not that difficult, it's just a very different mindset you have to get into, i.e. that of a ten-year-old boy, and have fun with it and not take yourself too seriously. I used to skive off school at St Brendan's sometimes, with a friend of mine, Ernest Johnson, and whenever I'd get nervous about it, he'd say, "What'll it matter in a hundred years' time?" That's my attitude to blockbusters like this.'

But that wasn't the only time when his past would

influence the present. Earlier in the shoot he had received the promised script of Steve McQueen's new movie. And it was a shocker.

CHAPTER FOURTEEN

A SHAMEFUL AFFAIR

Since his initial chat with Steve about his movie project with Abi Morgan about a sex addict, Michael had occasionally wondered what he had let himself in for after immediately saying that he wanted to be in it.

'Obviously when he told me what the subject was about, my imagination started to do its thing, so I was prepared for compromising positions and nudity and all that but I was a bit worried that I'd perhaps bitten off more than I could chew,' he admitted. But he trusted Steve and knew that it was an important story to tell. Also, the controversial nature of the film appealed to Michael's sense of danger and of wanting to keep people – including himself – guessing about what he might do next. He never wanted to feel too comfortable as an actor and, with the movie's numerous full-frontal nude scenes, he wasn't about to be disappointed on that score.

Unusually it was to be an entirely British made film, financed by Film Four and the UK Film Council and produced by Iain Canning and Emile Sherman, who later went on to produce *The King's Speech*. It was to be called *Shame* – the overriding feeling that sex addicts feel about their condition – but to Michael's relief, his first thought on reading the script was how beautifully written it was. He found that he really cared about the people in the story and thought that a reflection of Steve, who, he feels, really cares about human beings.

Michael was to play the lead role of sex addict Brandon with Carey Mulligan, who had co-starred with him in *Trial & Retribution* (and had since featured in *An Education* and *Drive*) playing his younger sister, Sissy. Steve and Abi's first thoughts were to set the story in London but, when they tried to speak to sex addicts as part of their research, they had a problem getting anyone to open up to them. Then Steve heard about two women in New York who had studied sex addiction and they introduced him and Abi to several people with this affliction.

'There was one guy – his wife was a very beautiful woman but there were a thousand other people he'd rather sleep with,' Steve recalled. 'It's the availability of sex. It's like there's more fatty food in supermarkets, so people get fat. There's greater accessibility to alcohol, so guess what? More people get pissed. That's how it is. Everyone wants to get lost a little bit these days – and understandably so.'

In his conversations with sex addicts, Steve noticed the word 'shame' kept cropping up after they had indulged themselves and he knew that he had stumbled upon the perfect title. They also had a huge feeling of self-hatred.

While they were in New York Steve decided to shoot the movie there. The story centres on Brandon – a thirty-something advertising executive who lives alone in a stylish, minimalist New York apartment. Handsome, successful and wealthy he may be but he is not in control of his life. His every move, every hour and seemingly every minute is consumed by his overwhelming obsession with sex. Each time he sees an attractive woman on the street, subway or in a bar, his head is turned and there is a leer on his face. At home and at work he accesses pornography on the Internet, hires prostitutes and picks up women – and the occasional man – in bars for instant sexual gratification. It leaves him feeling cold and unhappy but he seems unable to change or control his behaviour. Beneath the veneer of success he is a haunted, lonely man and his life becomes even more complicated when his wayward and emotionally unstable sister, Sissy, comes to stay with him.

Steve felt certain that the people he spoke to in New York were definitely addicted to sex and that the Internet made it easier for them to find self-gratification. 'In my day, the only access you had to pornography was the top shelf of a newsagent. Now you can click a mouse and get porn at any time of the day. So the Internet was very important in depicting the apparatus of a sex addict. Again, it is access to anything you want any time of day. Brandon is not at all exotic or a freak – he's one of us.'

Michael also chatted to sex addicts and, although at first he was unsure about the reality of the condition, he, like Steve, was left in no doubt that it was a genuine one. 'I didn't really know much about it at first. The first I'd heard about sex addiction was celebrities and I suppose there's the idea that they are spoiled and there's a lot of choice there and that, if anybody had the chance, they would be indulging in the same way. But having spoken to people and researched it, I am without a doubt sure that it is a real condition. It's happening and people's lives are being devastated by it. It's all consuming. There's this idea of the city being twenty-four/seven and that whatever you're into, it's there in some form or other.'

But it was the fact that people are ashamed to talk about it as if it were any other addiction, and thus unable to get help, that fascinated Michael. 'Initially you might laugh at the idea of sexual addiction but it becomes very serious pretty quickly when you see the devastation that it leaves in its wake. There seems to be some kind of stigma about it. It seems more acceptable to deal with alcohol or drug addiction. What's interesting is that drugs or alcohol are outside influences that you bring in, whereas sex is within us. It's something that's innately there and is part of our make-up and instinct, so when that becomes imbalanced and reaches an unhealthy situation, what do you do with it? Do you totally abstain, or do you try to negotiate life?'

In the end Michael focused on one particular man for his portrayal of Brandon. 'I was very grateful that somebody was open enough and brave enough to give me an insight into it. Then it was a matter of treating it with the utmost respect and not hiding behind certain characters or caricatures of any sort. I tried to keep it as close to me as possible so that it was relevant to me, just as it could be to any regular guy on the street.'

Brandon has problems with intimacy because he doesn't feel in control of such things. This makes him lonely and destructive. He's a complex character and one that Michael, as an actor, enjoyed trying to understand. 'Most men think about sex a lot. We know that. But for someone like Brandon it is a compulsion. That's where the shame comes in: you're no longer in control of your choices.'

The only woman Brandon finds attractive but cannot treat in his predatory, love-'em-and-leave-'em way is his work colleague Marianne (Nicole Beharie). The two go on a date where she teases him about his lack of commitment in relationships, the longest of which has lasted just four months. Later, to Brandon's shock, he is unable to sexually perform with her in bed.

In an interview with the *Irish Independent*, he opened up a little about his own personal life. 'I could relate to certain elements of Brandon. A lot of guy friends I've spoken to since then have said the same thing. But what has really struck me is how grateful I am to have a healthy relationship with sex and my own sexual life. I like intimacy, whereas Brandon flinches at the notion. There's no gratification in his sexual acts. It's just a compulsion, with no nourishment or pleasure.'

The shoot on *X-Men: First Class* ran a little over schedule, cutting into Michael's precious preparation time. This was always very intense and comprehensive and he felt that he particularly needed it for a complex man like Brandon in *Shame*. An interview with *Dazed & Confused* magazine gave some insight into his technique. 'When dealing with any fictional character I write a biography,' he explained. 'That's simply to give me a confidence within the character and what he's going through in the here and now. That's one of the first things I do: What did his parents do? What was he like in school? What does he have for breakfast? Whatever the questions are. Those are the kind of things that goes into the preparation.

'I spent a lot of time with the script, reading and re-reading it. So through that I get to understand the rhythms of the text and the rhythms of the character, the physical life of the character. You just try to find it in yourself. But most of it, though, is down to me working with the script, working with the dialogue and understanding the character. All these things start to seep into your enamel. That's the system I do with every job.'

In another interview, he compared his approach to that of a sportsman getting to the top of his profession through constant practice. 'Look, there are no secrets to anything in life. Tiger Woods is Tiger Woods because he practised that fucking swing a hundred times a day. Why should acting be any different? It's just boring repetition and, through that, I find things start to break down and you start to find the nuances, all the interesting little details.'

But his *X-Men* commitment meant that his time was limited. They had just five weeks to film it and so he busily immersed himself in the script, doing his usual re-reading during filming and learning more about the character and his inner demons as he went along.

Michael also took time out in between finishing *X-Men: First Class* and focusing on *Shame* to attend a special tribute to the British producer Jeremy Thomas, arranged by the Academy of Motion Picture Arts & Sciences at the Curzon Theatre in London on 25 November. Jeremy, whose father Ralph had directed the *Doctor...* series of comedies and whose uncle Gerald the *Carry On* movies, had won an Oscar in 1988 for *The Last Emperor*, the first of his many collaborations with Bernardo Bertolucci.

Tom Conti, who had starred in Jeremy's 1983 production *Merry Christmas Mr Lawrence*, hosted the evening of spoken tributes, film clips, video messages and conversation covering Jeremy's 40-year career. Michael introduced the first footage from *A Dangerous Method*, for which Jeremy had acted as producer.

Michael also managed to squeeze in three days of filming on John Maclean's second short movie, *Pitch Black Heist*, which saw him team up again with Liam Cunningham as two crooks who try to break into an office safe. But the presence of a light-activated alarm system means they have to do it in darkness. Despite John having a bigger budget this time, it was still made for less than £30,000 and the blacked-out screen used for the final part of the 13-minute film was a canny cost-saving ploy. Most of the short was filmed at the house of a friend and the dialogue was recorded later. The rest of it, featuring the two thieves discussing the robbery in a pub, was shot at The Dolphin in Hackney, near where Michael lives.

Despite being intrigued by the subject matter of *Shame* and excited by the prospect of working with Steve again, Michael was not looking forward to baring all on screen. 'I was self-conscious, for sure, but it was something I had to get over very quickly,' he said. 'Those scenes are really where you get an insight into the guy's psyche. When you see him naked, it's in more ways than one. So by concentrating on that you get over the fact that you're stark bollock naked. It's not that big a deal anyway. A proportion of us in the human race have penises and another proportion of them have seen them, whether they be mothers, girlfriends or partners or whatever, so I don't know why it's so unusual to show that in a movie.'

Further, he reasoned, women had been stripping off in movies for years and it was about time the tables were turned. 'For women it must be refreshing to not always have to see women parading around naked while the guy always has his pants on.'

Michael also argued that there was far less of a commotion about violence in film than sex and nudity, saying that it seems to be more the norm to have a gun in your hand and shooting somebody. He was more concerned about the welfare of the actresses with whom he shared the sex scenes than his own anxieties. 'You try to make sure that your partner in the scene is comfortable. I'd say, "Let's go for it now and it'll be over soon." It sounds terrible, like a really bad chat-up line!' he said with a laugh.

Carey Mulligan thought Michael had been brave to take on the role. 'A lot of actors, especially when they are as talented and good looking as Michael, only want parts where they are shown in a good light,' she told the *Irish Examiner*. 'If I learned anything working with Michael, it's that he's utterly fearless.'

Michael returned the compliment to Carey. 'She was very easy to work with because she was brave, throwing herself into the mix. When you're working with Steve it can be quite a frightening experience but also very exciting and educational because there are no safety rails and nowhere to hide.'

Carey admitted to being nervous working with Michael because she admired him so much as an actor. 'It was quite scary because I've watched him and looked up to him for years and so it was like working with one of my idols. But he's great. He makes you feel so comfortable and he's very supportive.'

Interestingly, they decided not to socialise outside of filming because the characters they were playing were at loggerheads with each other and the two actors felt it would help their work if they didn't become too friendly.

Working with Steve may be a 'frightening experience' (in Michael's words) but it was always exhilarating and the bond between the two men was becoming ever stronger. Both wanted to work with each other more than anything else and there was a very real mutual respect. 'I really consider Steve to be a genius. I know that's a word that gets bandied around but when I met him, I knew it was a life-changing moment for me,' said Michael. 'He's a great leader. He inspires people. When we were making *Hunger*, he worked with such passion. I could see it so clearly on people's faces, the joy of coming to work every day. In New York, shooting *Shame*, I saw the same thing again. People want to do their very best for him. They don't want to let him down.'

Michael also appreciated Steve's humility and no-nonsense approach to life. Despite the fact that Michael knew nothing about the art world, he said that Steve never made him feel inadequate or stupid. 'There's something very old-school mannerly about him. I've really found my teacher in Steve and hopefully he's found an apprentice in me,' he told the *Hollywood Reporter*.

One of those 'frightening experiences' occurred early on in the shoot when after a particularly intense scene Michael commented, 'Yeah, that's pretty good for a first take. You know, not bad.'

Steve looked at him and said, 'Let's have a chat.' They then went into a separate room where Steve told him, 'Some actor geezer just came into the room here. That wasn't Michael Fassbender. I know what you're doing but you've got to find something different.'

'I was like, "Oh, shit,"' Michael recalled. 'So I went back to the drawing board and tried to pare things down and just make them honest.'

During a break in filming he told *Total Film* magazine, 'I'm spending a lot of time with the character and getting to know him. So throughout the day I'll think, "What would Brandon do in this scenario?" It's about trying to understand and relate to him, as opposed to judging. That would be a mistake.'

The restaurant scene is perhaps the only charming one in the movie, showing the awkwardness, the pauses and flirtation of a first date. Initially there were pages of dialogue for the actors but, when they were ready to shoot it, Steve suggested that they improvise much of the dialogue to make it seem more realistic. When Brandon and Marianne are walking back after their date, he asks her which era she would most like to live in. When it's his turn to answer, Michael expresses his own private fantasy that he has always wanted to be a musician in the 1960s.

The bedroom scene was actually shot before the one in the restaurant. Nicole had been dreading it and was very relieved by how supportive and understanding Michael was. 'I just tried to pretend there wasn't a camera in the room,' she said. 'Michael is so engaged and so much fun to work with. I know I couldn't have gotten through that scene without him. He is a total gentleman.'

Michael had always hoped to find a director as in tune with his ideas as Steve and considered himself extremely fortunate to have done so. For his part, Steve, a big, imposing man, with a rather stern default expression, talked about Michael as he might a lover in some newspaper interviews. 'With Michael I've actually met someone with whom I have some kind of link,' he told *The Times*. 'It's odd. Strange. And I never saw it coming. It was never a thing for which I strived. But when you find someone, it's like falling in love. You want to keep it. And I think myself and Michael are very pleased that we've found each other in that way.'

His praise for Michael's acting ability knew no bounds and he put him firmly up there with the all-time greats – and Michael's heroes. 'There is no one like Michael out there right now. And there hasn't been, for me, since Marlon Brando. There's a fragility and femininity to him, but also a masculinity that can translate. You're not in awe of him. You're part of him. He pulls you in. And that's what you want from an actor. You want people to look at him and see themselves.'

During a break in filming to promote *Jane Eyre*, Michael modestly brushed aside a journalist from the *Irish Voice Reporter* who mentioned his impressive list of film credits. 'Oh, Jesus, it's all luck and timing,' he said. 'I think you have to be aware of when your opportunities are coming. When *Hunger* came my way I just knew I had to get that one right. I was being given a chance to get my foot in the door. I think being aware of that and seizing it when it's there helped. That feeling of timing is really important in this business, definitely. Having business awareness is important too.'

When he wasn't flying around the world making and promoting movies, Michael was now happily settled in the East End of London. Although he had enjoyed the weather and creativity of Los Angeles, he found the necessity of driving everywhere rather than walking odd. He preferred the buzz of New York – one of his favourite cities – where he could walk the streets and enjoy the sights and sounds. This was the type of thing he loved doing in London.

In an interview with the fan website, *fassinatingfassbender.com*, he told how he likes to keep upbeat and talk to and smile at people he sees throughout the day. 'That interaction with people, and getting on the tube in the morning and buying your ticket… If you have a little conversation with the person who is giving you the ticket, smile and ask how their day is going, that sort of perks them up a little. And that exchange makes me feel good then to start my day off, you know. I think it's likewise for most people, you know that interaction, it keeps us going.'

When he was making it in the business, it had been New York that symbolised the dream of being an actor. He told the French magazine *Obsession* that his acting method had come from the books and writings of Stanislavski and Lee Strasberg, the whole school of the Actors Studio. But as he couldn't afford to live in New York he had settled in London instead. But that, too, had proved very expensive and he'd had to keep finding cheaper accommodation. Now that he was in much better financial shape he was rediscovering the joys of living in London compared to car-bound LA or the frenetic pace of New York. 'It's a place where you can take your time. I need to walk the streets and see the seasons change and not have endless sunshine.'

He expanded on the subject to *Radio Times* magazine: 'I love London. I love its diversity, the wonderful mix of people. I love the fact that I can afford to take the tube without worrying about it. I keep an eye on the money I make because it's important for me to make sure that I don't go back to counting every 50p. If you can survive in London, you can survive anywhere.'

Now, after an intense five weeks of filming on *Shame*, he was looking to relax. He had enjoyed the experience of playing Brandon but it had left him drained. It had been the toughest job of his life, he admitted, and from someone who had starved himself to play a hunger protester, that was no lightweight remark. 'I enjoyed being honest with myself making the film and exploring those things that society has deemed to be shameful,' he said. 'I don't have the answers to a lot of the moral questions but it's important to pose them.'

However, he was quick to disperse any notions of him being the kind of actor who believed in suffering for his art. 'I don't want to be one of those actors who's sitting there saying, "This is such hard work," when obviously there's a lot of people out there doing proper hard graft,' he told the *Sunday Independent*. 'But the fact of the matter is that this was the fifth film of six films I did over a twenty-month period and they were all back-to-back so I was jumping from one personality to the next. By the time I got to *Shame*, I was kind of tired.'

Having made 5 films in just 12 months – *Haywire*, *Jane Eyre*, *A Dangerous Method*, *X-Men: First Class* and *Shame* – he had been looking forward to an extended rest. It had been a hectic period, diving from one project to the next and creatively exhilarating. But now it was time to sit back, take stock and enjoy some downtime. That was the plan. But then, to paraphrase one of his heroes, Marlon Brando in *The Godfather*, he was made an offer that he couldn't refuse.

CHAPTER FIFTEEN

SPACED OUT

Sir Ridley Scott, whose directorial credits include *Blade Runner*, *Thelma and Louise*, *Black Rain* and *Gladiator*, had contacted Michael during the filming of *Shame* to say that he would like him in his latest movie, *Prometheus*. Despite feeling jaded after a run of back-to-back movies, Michael knew he couldn't turn down the chance to work with such an acclaimed director. He would do one more film and *then* take a break.

It was to be another blockbuster movie, and rumoured to be a prequel to Scott's 1979 sci-fi classic, *Alien*. The story follows the crew of the spaceship *Prometheus* in the year 2085, as they explore an advanced alien civilisation to uncover the origins of humanity. Michael was to play a lifelike human android named David, the latest creation of the Weyland-Yutani Corporation, headed by Peter Weyland (Guy Pearce). Swedish actress Noomi Rapace was to play archaeologist and scientist Elizabeth Shaw after Scott had been impressed by her performance as Lisbeth Salander in *The Girl With the Dragon Tattoo*.

Charlize Theron was cast as Meredith Vickers, Weyland's company rep on the spaceship, captained by Janek (Idris Elba). The other crew were Logan Marshall-Green (best known for his TV roles in *24* and *The O.C.* and the movies *Devil* and *Brooklyn's Finest*) as hot-headed scientist Charlie Holloway, Rafe Spall (*Hot Fuzz*, *Shaun of the Dead*) as botanist Milburn and Sean Harris (*Brighton Rock*, *Harry Brown*) as geologist Fifield.

Michael was fascinated by David, by his multiple functions as butler, housekeeper and maintenance man aboard the spaceship, and by the way the crew treated him. Because he is not human he routinely fails to get any respect and his superior intellect and advanced physicality gives rise to some contempt. This brought in the intriguing notion of how David would feel about the crew over time. Is he capable of emotions? What if he started to develop human personality traits? For two and a half years the crew are in cryostatis – a sleeping state – so David matures differently over that period of time. What does he do to amuse himself?

News of *Prometheus* caused a big stir among fans of *Alien*. Ridley was determined to keep details of the script from being leaked, so secrecy was paramount. The cast had to sign clauses forbidding disclosure of story details and their first reading of the script was under supervision in Ridley's production office.

Michael was impressed, thinking the script intelligent, well constructed and respectful of the lineage of the story. 'It was a real thriller with real anticipation. *Alien* had that. The atmosphere was thick. You knew that something was going to happen. It's very rare that you can read that in a script.' By way of preparation, he chose not to revisit *Alien* or its sequels, *Aliens*, *Alien 3* and *Alien Resurrection*, but instead watched one of his favourite Ridley Scott movies, *Blade Runner*.

His inspiration when it came to David's posture and movement was not an obvious one. He modelled him on the American Olympic diver, Greg Louganis. As for his behaviour and personality, Michel felt there should be an androgynous quality to David. With his hair dyed blond for the role – which, he remarked, made him look like 'a ten-quid rent boy' – he thought of TE Lawrence and David Bowie, who 'both have a feminine quality about them'.

He also joked to *Empire* magazine, 'I haven't suggested this to Ridley but I want David to be doing a robot dance, in a secret disco room on the ship. I want him sitting there with a disco ball and a floor that lights up!'

Filming began in March 2011 at Pinewood Studios in Buckinghamshire. 'It's the story of creation, the gods and the man who stood against them. It's not a small film,' commented Ridley to journalists. 'I'm using the giant James Bond 007 stage at Pinewood and six other sound stages to film it.' Other filming took place in Spain, Toronto and Iceland, where the first 15 minutes of the film unfold in a 'beginning of time' sequence.

Michael was dazzled by the big-budget effects. Walking on set, he said, was like walking on a spaceship with all the panels, screens and lights. Much of it was physically there rather than added later via CGI. Attention to detail was important, Ridley said, right down to the smallest of things – even shoelaces. 'There was even a big argument about the globular helmets,' he said. 'I was certain I wanted the fully spherical glass helmet. I'm in 2083 and I'm going to space – why would I design a helmet that has blind spots when what I want is a globular helmet, a three-sixty?'

Michael was also impressed by how unpretentious, accessible and available Ridley was to everyone on set, always willing to listen to ideas. Like other quality directors Michael had worked with, Ridley encouraged his actors to use their intuitive and interpretative skills as much as possible, rather than bluntly be told what to do. 'Ridley comes to you with an interesting prop and says, "I see your character maybe messing around with this,"' Michael explained to GQ magazine. 'It's just the oddest little things – like he might rub his finger on a desk to test for dust and then you're thinking "OK, right, that'll take me on a mental tangent."

'That's the thing with all these directors – none of them want to give you a direct, "Just do this in the scene." They want you to find it by yourself. A great director is a great manipulator. They might manipulate you two nights before at a dinner by saying a phrase or by mentioning a piece of information that you realise when you come on set, "Ah, that's what they're talking about." You don't even realise they're doing it.'

The glasses that Ridley wanted Rafe Spall to wear as Millburn, however, caused much amusement among the cast after Rafe said that they made him look like Dame Edna Everage!

Screenwriter Damon Lindelof (whose credits include the TV series *Lost* and the offbeat Daniel Craig-Harrison Ford movie *Cowboys & Aliens*) remarked on how impressed he was by eager fans of *Alien*.

I've been astonished by the patience of the fan base in terms of how little we're telling them about the movie. There does seem to be this dance we're doing together where people want to know more about it and we say, 'Do you really want to know?' and they say, 'No no no no no! We don't! We actually just want to go into the movie not knowing if there's a bomb under the table or not or when it's going to go off.'

Ridley has always had a tremendous amount of faith in the audience's intelligence and he directs in a way and tells stories in a way that you come up to them, as opposed to it talks down to you. I feel like *Prometheus* is a proud member of that thing he does so well.

Damon also felt that the film tapped in to how humans would view exploring space in the years to come. 'Space exploration in the future is going to evolve into this idea that it's not just about going out there and finding planets to build colonies,' he said. 'It also has this inherent idea that the further we go out, the more we learn about ourselves. The characters in this movie are preoccupied by the idea: what are our origins?'

After filming wrapped at the end of July, Michael finally took his overdue break. He had been looking forward to a holiday at one of his favourite holiday destinations – Trancoso in Brazil with its beautiful white beaches. 'I love the Brazilian temperament,' he has said. 'Everything is very sexy. They do everything better and sexier than we do. There's a spirit of joy and living life that's very infectious and nice to be around.'

A keen world traveller, Michael enjoys meeting people and experiencing different cultures. Often he will pop into a church on his travels and light a candle but he drifted away from Catholicism years ago – 'too many contradictions'. However, he still respects priests and sees them as figures of authority so he was chastened when he wandered into a church in Germany and was told off by the priest for wearing a hat. 'My grandfather would have been very cross,' he later remarked. 'He believed that if you entered any building at all, you took your hat off.'

When *X-Men: First Class* opened in June 2011 it was a critical and box-office smash. Michael, in particular, was picked out for attention. He had entered the big-studio movie world without shedding his credibility and it sent his star appeal soaring. In playing Magneto he had managed to avoid a one-dimensional, comic-book caricature in which a super-power and a cool outfit zapped gravitas and emotional inner struggles. Michael's portrayal was of a real man with real anxieties, which allowed even non-fans of the genre to enjoy his performance and the movie.

The *Sun* raved, 'In every sense this is genuinely First Class.' The *Telegraph* smelled an instant hit. 'In a summer movie season that promises to be dominated by superheroes and special effects, a group of mutants and telepaths are set to rule the box office,' it said, adding, 'It's not your average superhero movie.'

As well as describing it as a 'rip-roaringly enjoyable action prequel', the *Daily Mirror* echoed Michael's thoughts. 'It doesn't feel like a superhero movie, being more interested in the characters struggling with their outsider status than KAPOW! moments,' it said. 'You don't get people this rounded in your standard Oscar flick. And, if it doesn't feel like a typical superhero movie, it doesn't look like one either, more closely resembling an early James Bond film.'

The *Independent on Sunday* also picked up on the Bond theme. 'The young Magneto (Ian McKellen in the first films) is a dashing Nazi-hunter played by Michael Fassbender with more than a dash of James Bond and Harry Palmer.' The *Daily Express* agreed: 'Sleek, charismatic Fassbender shows us what a perfect Bond he could be.'

Several critics thought the film revitalised the X-Men series. The *Daily Express* said, '*First Class* takes the X-Men story back to its roots and is just the kick in the pants the series needed. It is smart, spectacular, never cheesy, often thrilling and always incredibly entertaining.' The *Telegraph* concurred that it was 'a stylish, snappy reboot to the Marvel comics series', although it did criticise Michael's accent for 'being all over the place'. In America, *USA Today* said the movie 'revives the flagging franchise with this globe-trotting iteration, infusing it with new life and dazzling visual effects'.

In all, it was generally agreed that Michael's performance stood out among a good cast. The *New York Post* raved, 'A large and talented cast manages to make more than a dozen characters pop, but still this is the Michael Fassbender show. He was a wonder as Bobby Sands in *Hunger* and showed huge charisma in *Basterds*. Now he's where Christian Bale was about six years ago, a fresh, silky menace ready to fill any helmet or fire any weapon you've got.'

The *Washington Post* agreed: 'In all honesty, *First Class* belongs to one actor, and that's Fassbender, whose Erik/Magneto emerges as one of the most nuanced, conflicted, genuinely antiheroic protagonists in recent comic-book-movie memory. As a transparent and eminently watchable vessel for contradictory impulses – vulnerability and superhuman strength, victimization and destruction, discipline and reckless rage – Fassbender's Magneto is not unlike Bobby Sands, the IRA activist he portrayed in the 2008 film *Hunger*. His penultimate set piece, when Magneto singlehandedly raises a submarine out of deep waters through sheer force of his will, is one of those rare instances when an authentic screen performance isn't drowned out by sheer spectacle.'

Entertainment Weekly, meanwhile, was very taken with Michael and James McAvoy's partnership. 'McAvoy and Fassbender are a casting triumph. These two have, yes, real star magnetism, both individually and together. They're both cool and intense, suave and unaffected, playful and dead serious about their grand comic-book work.'

Back home, Josef was amazed and proud of his son's career success and impressed by the top-drawer people he had got to work with. 'For him to be working with big actors, all the top guns... we never thought we would see this day. It's great. You can see he enjoys what he does,' he told the *Irish Independent*.

But what about his future? With most of the *First Class* story set at the height of the Cold War and an evil megalomaniac out to conquer the world, Michael's cold and ruthless portrayal of Magneto (not to mention the bespoke 1960s clothes) had had quite a few critics thinking of him as the next James Bond.

When the *IndieLondon* website asked him if he'd be interested in playing 007, Michael replied, 'Well, it's very flattering of course and Matthew [Vaughn] had sort of mentioned in some of the earlier meetings that it [the film] did evoke a lot of memories for him of those earlier Bond films. But for me in terms of approaching the character of Erik, I didn't really go along that route. I mean, they dressed me up in clothes and bespoke suits that sort of harked back to those early Bond films but I really just approached it through the material that was available from the comic books. In terms of what I might expect or be hoping for in the future... I never try and plan anything. I never expect anything. I think Daniel [Craig] is doing a fantastic job, so let's just deal with this film at the moment and see how that turns out.'

He told other reporters, 'Honestly, I've heard a lot of stories but nothing has been brought officially to me. It's a huge honour to even be associated with the [Bond] movies and I'd be lying if I said I wasn't flattered. If anything did ever happen – in my wildest dreams, of course – it would make me the first ginger Bond! Some people did kick up about Daniel Craig being the first blond 007 but I wonder how they would feel about a red-headed one instead.'

But speculation and rumour only intensified after Daniel Craig himself gave Michael his seal of approval a few weeks later. In an interview with the *Irish Sun*, he said, 'Without a shadow of a doubt, the role is Michael's. Honestly, he has my blessing. I've met him a couple of times and he's just such a brilliant actor with a phenomenal presence. If he's up for it, I think he'd be a perfect fit for the part. You can see him as 007 – he has all the right traits. It's meant to be. I'm also a big fan of his work so I'd happily pass the torch to him, whenever that will be.'

CHAPTER SIXTEEN

EASY RIDER

N ow with time to unwind, Michael – a big Formula 1 racing fan – was invited by the Red Bull team to watch the British F1 Grand Prix at Silverstone, Northamptonshire, along with actress Gemma Arterton and rapper Goldie.

In an interview with Jeremy Clarkson, host of BBC1's *Top Gear*, he admitted being star-struck when he spotted his hero, Michael Schumacher, emerging from the Mercedes garage. 'I ran behind him like a stalker calling, "Schumacher, Schumacher," and he kept walking. So I was like, "Michael!" He stopped and I shook his hand and said, "I still think you're the best." And he looked at me with a bit of a smile but with fear in his eyes. So I did get the chance to meet him but he didn't know who the hell I was!'

When it comes to speed, Michael usually gets his thrills behind the wheel of a go-kart, which he describes as his favourite pastime. He also loves travelling long distances on his motorbike, a BMW 1200 GS Adventure, which he bought after his Triumph Speed Triple was stolen. 'You get to clear your head there. It's a brilliant, freeing thing to do,' he told Clarkson. In similar vein, he talked to the French magazine, *Obsession*, about life on the road as being a 'cathartic experience' where there was a great feeling of camaraderie between fellow bikers.

That summer Michael took the opportunity to do something he had first talked about with his dad 10 years ago – travel across Europe on a motorbike. When he first mentioned it, he didn't even have a motorbike or a licence but it was something that father and son both thought, 'one day'. After he had finished on *Prometheus*, he really wanted a break and told Josef, 'This could happen, so be ready to move.' After some hasty planning he asked his father if he still fancied it and Josef was as enthusiastic as his son. 'Hats off to him, he's as tough as nails,' Michael told the *Radio Times*.

With Michael on his BMW and Josef on a Triumph Tiger, the pair set off on a 3,000-mile motorcycling holiday across Europe for 2 months. Back home Adele was worried about Josef – with good cause, it seems, because both he and Michael narrowly avoided a serious accident on two separate occasions. 'At one point I was sandwiched between two speeding cars and I could feel the rush of wind as one missed me by a whisker,' Michael recalled. 'Another time he [Josef] nudged out onto a road and looked right but the car was coming from the left and again it was inches away. But thank God, it was all fine.'

Michael turned his phone off for most of the time and enjoyed the freedom of getting away from it all. He and his 'road mate' took plenty of time visiting the towns and villages along the way. Although he was occasionally recognised, it was never more than somebody saying that they enjoyed his work, so it was a hassle-free trip that recharged the batteries.

After travelling through Holland, Germany, Austria, Slovenia, Croatia, Bosnia and Montenegro, the two of them arrived in Italy. There they visited Sicily, Sorrento, Rome, Florence and Lake Garda before arriving in Venice in time for the Film Festival at the start of September. Both *Shame* and *A Dangerous Method* were being premiered there, amid a strong year for British films. *Shame*, Andrea Arnold's *Wuthering Heights* and Tomas Alfredson's *Tinker Tailor Soldier Spy* turned out to be three of the best reviewed and most talked about.

Michael's mother, Adele, was due to fly in to join them in Venice for the screening of *Shame* but a back injury meant that she had to stay at home instead. Michael later joked that the injury might have been 'psychosomatic' because she wasn't keen to see her son naked in sex scenes. Michael had warned his father that there was going to be 'some pretty extreme stuff' and to prepare himself and Josef had replied, 'Look, you are an artist and you have got to do your thing.' But as the audience sat in engrossed silence watching the stark film play out on the screen, Josef leaned towards his son and whispered, 'Thank God your mother isn't here.'

At the end of the movie there was a seven-minute standing ovation. It was the first time that Michael had watched the film and he admitted to feeling odd, sitting there knowing that everyone had seen him naked.

David Cronenberg, who was also in Venice, marvelled at how Michael was able to look different in each film and hardly be recognised off screen. After a screening of *A Dangerous Method*, he recalled that nobody recognised Michael until he was introduced to the audience. The director thought this 'chameleon' quality rare and one of Michael's great skills. Even back home in Hackney people rarely recognised him or, if they did, were pleasant and didn't bother him and he loved that.

When asked by the *Irish Examiner* how he coped with celebrity, he replied, 'None of the trappings of fame really interest me. Ten years ago I would have been very impressed and seduced by all the things that come with it but it doesn't interest me now.' He was also niggled by the fact that, once you were successful and financially secure, people gave you things for free. It made him think, 'Why didn't you give me that free suit ten years ago when I couldn't afford to get a bus?'

Shame was hotly tipped to win the prize for Best Film but Michael was star-struck by the glamour around him and couldn't believe how far he had come in his career. It was the first time he had been to Venice and sitting on a balcony with family and friends, relaxing with a drink and soaking up the atmosphere was one of the most enjoyable moments in his life. Even one of his biggest heroes, Al Pacino, was there and he had to pinch himself to check that it was all for real.

Things were to get even more dream-like. On the closing day of the festival Michael was preparing to fly to the Toronto International Film Festival when word reached him that it might be worth his while to stick around. He hastily postponed the flight and – like a plot from a cheesy movie – arrived at the Sala Grande on the Venice Lido with just 15 minutes to spare before he heard his name called out as winner of the Best Actor prize for *Shame*.

A beaming Michael walked on stage and said to the audience, '*Buona sera, Venezia. Grazie mille.* It's really nice when you take a chance and do something and you think it's relevant, and you hope it's relevant, and people respond the way they did. So, thank you very much, once again, to Steve McQueen – my hero. And also I'd like to say it's a real privilege to be in and among the other films, film-makers and actors that have been here at this festival. It's such a wonderful tradition. *Grazie mille.*'

Later, Michael paid tribute to another of his acting heroes who was at the festival, Gary Oldman, who had played British spy George Smiley in *Tinker Tailor Soldier Spy*. After saying that he had been following Gary's career since he was 14 and that he 'blows my mind', he added that he felt very humble tonight. When told what Michael had said about him by journalists present, Gary replied, 'I think he's the bollocks. The real deal. When I heard what he'd said about me, I thought, "Here's back at you, kid."'

Shame lost out in the Best Film category to the Russian film, *Faust*, directed by Aleksandr Sokurov, but the jury president, US director Darren Aronofsky, paid special tribute to it, saying, 'We were blown away by *Shame* and the cinematic power of it.'

The following day Michael flew with Steve McQueen to Toronto, where he was reunited with his girlfriend, Zoe Kravitz. The pair attended a movie party at Grey Goose Soho House, where – in the top floor recreation room – Michael enjoyed a game of table tennis with the American actor Justin Long, who was in town for the screening of his movie, *Ten Year*. Michael and Zoe also attended the prestigious Creative Artists Agency party at the Burroughes Building, where he was congratulated on his success at Venice by the likes of Colin Farrell, Clive Owen, Gerard Butler and Ethan Hawke.

Come the festival itself, *Shame* was watched in stunned silence by the audience, followed by rapturous applause. Later, Michael told a Canadian interviewer that he didn't care about choosing roles to suit any kind of perceived image that he had, nor did he think of himself as a commodity. 'It's my job to go to places that are uncomfortable to go to, or to push the envelope, so that an audience member can vicariously take that journey with me, and ask questions, serious questions of themselves,' he said. But, worried about sounding too precious, he smiled and added, '...as well as doing more popcorn-driven films.'

He also underlined that he was taking the rest of the year off to 'clear the decks' and because he didn't want to 'bore everybody'.

Meanwhile, *Jane Eyre* had been released to generally excellent reviews. 'Cool, temperate, finely wrought, this new adaptation of Charlotte Bronte's *Jane Eyre* is enclosed in a crinoline of intelligent good taste,' said The *Guardian*, adding, 'Michael Fassbender plays Rochester with a measured, observant intensity.' The critic from *USA Today* agreed: 'Michael Fassbender powerfully portrays the surliness of the tormented Mr Rochester.'

Michael and Mia's on screen relationship worked for most. 'Mia Wasikowska and Michael Fassbender breathe new life into Charlotte Bronte's drama of love and loss in this surprisingly unmelodramatic and sparse costume drama,' said the *Sun*. 'A beautifully elegant re-telling of Charlotte Bronte's classic with the protagonists moody and moving,' said the *Sunday Mirror*. 'I'm inclined to say that the Wasikowska/Fassbender duet puts all others to shame – they are leaps and bounds better than Orson

Welles and Joan Fontaine in the 1944 film,' said the *Daily Telegraph,* adding, 'Fassbender, imposing as ever, has a feral quality that makes his handsomeness dangerous.'

The *Observer,* however, couldn't agree. 'This *Jane Eyre* is a good-looking film, serious, thought through and well acted,' it admitted. 'Yet it ends up rather shallow, lacking the cinematic intensity of the Orson Welles version, though that was widely patronised and sneered at in its day.'

For its part, *Total Film* magazine couldn't leave the subject of James Bond alone: 'As Rochester, Fassbender again shows he's one of his generation's most virile, compelling leading men, in a role (previously played, lest we forget, by one Timothy Dalton) that will do his chances of landing Bond no harm at all.'

After flying back to Venice to pick up his bike, Michael continued his road trip on his own, through the French Alps and Barcelona and arriving in San Sebastian for the Film Festival on 23 September. He caused quite a stir in his biking leathers as he pulled up outside the Maria Cristina Hotel, where he gave interviews with the Spanish media to promote *Shame.*

At the festival, Steve McQueen received a Special Recognition award from the Youth Jury, made up of young Spanish film students. Michael presented the trophy for Best European Film to Nadine Labaki's *Where Do We Go Now?* then memorably showed off his vocal talents at the closing ceremony. As a parade of leading lights took the microphone in turn onstage at the Kursaal

Palace to say a brief farewell, he surprised everyone by singing the Sinatra favourite *Summer Wind* – a fond look back at a fleeting romance – to generous applause. The following day he was back on his bike, travelling to Biarritz before finally heading home to London, travelling about 5,000 miles in all.

Michael might have taken a break from making films but the promotional carousel continued at a pace. On 24 October he attended the premiere for *A Dangerous Method* at the BFI London Film Festival at the Odeon West End in London with co-stars Keira Knightley, Viggo Mortensen and director David Cronenberg. But it wasn't long before he was out of the country again. On 6 November a special screening of *Haywire* caused a buzz at the American Film Institute Festival in Los Angeles, where Michael was reunited with his co-stars Ewan McGregor and Gina Carano at Grauman's Chinese Theater on Hollywood Boulevard.

Then he was off to *GQ* magazine's annual Men of the Year party at the luxury Chateau Marmont in West Hollywood, where he was named Break-out Star of the Year. He also brought along his new girlfriend.

CHAPTER SEVENTEEN

SHAMELESS LOVE

As quietly as he had begun dating her, Michael signalled that his relationship with Zoe Kravitz had come to an end when he invited his new love to Chateau Marmont. The pair arrived separately but, no matter how discreet he liked to be about his love life, there was no hiding the fact that the pair had already been seen naked in bed together – by millions around the world.

Michael was besieged by autograph hunters as he arrived, wearing a black suit and white open-necked shirt. Patiently he took the time to sign his name again and again but it was rather like King Canute trying to hold back the tide and it was some time before he made it inside the building. Once there, he smoked a cigar as he mingled with other guests – including Justin Timberlake, Jessica Biel, Nicole Sherzinger and Jay-Z – with his arm around the waist of his date, his *Shame* co-star Nicole Beharie.

Michael told an interviewer for *GQ* magazine outside that his job was to facilitate characters in a story so a pat on the back was a nice feeling. He added that he was flattered to be in the company of the likes of Jay-Z because he was a big fan of his. When asked what he would have liked to do if it were not for acting, he laughed and said that his first dream was to be a musician but he wasn't good enough. He had also wanted to be a war journalist, being on the front line, 'getting an unfiltered account of what's going on in these places'.

That month – November – Michael was the cover of *GQ*, which carried an interview with him. In it he was a little more outspoken about his private life than normal, saying that he liked the idea of settling down and raising a family but thought it would be difficult for a partner to cope with the demands of his job. 'I'm quite a romantic person and I love the idea of having a family but I'd have to take a step back out of this,' he said. 'It's not fair on somebody to be waiting for you. You spend long periods of time apart and then when I am here [in the UK] I am working. I find it difficult to do both and to give that other person the right amount of attention and time they deserve.'

He conceded, too, that actors don't have a reputation for staying faithful. 'I don't think it's a cliché. You're travelling around a lot and perhaps lonely and you want some kind of connection again. You're in a position where people treat you differently. They are living what appears to be an attractive lifestyle. Your opportunities are multiplied again, so there's a buffet of choice.'

Asked what he looks for in a woman, he replied, 'Intelligence, self-confidence in one's own skin. If a girl is slightly overweight or, you know, if she's comfortable in herself, living life the way she wants to live it, I find that sexy and attractive. If somebody is the perfect mould but she's not enjoying herself, I find it sad and unsexy.'

On 2 December, Michael collected yet another trophy – the Los Angeles Film Critics Award for Best Actor – and then it was the turn of the Moet Independent British Film Awards. The 2011 event took place on 4 December at Old Billingsgate in London and the stars in attendance included Vanessa Redgrave, Ralph Fiennes, Daniel Craig, Benedict Cumberbatch, Charles Dance, Gemma Arterton, Dominic Cooper, Emilia Fox, Kenneth Branagh and the American director, Ron Howard. *Shame* was nominated in six categories, including Best Film, Best Director, Best Screenplay and Best Supporting Actress, but only Michael was victorious on the night when he was voted Best Actor for his performance as Brandon.

Michael was being tipped for Academy Awards success too so he was delighted to be among the nominees for the Golden Globes –traditionally the weathervane for the Oscars – when they were announced on 14 December. In the Best Actor (Drama) category he was up against George Clooney for *The Descendents*, Brad Pitt for *Moneyball*, Leonardo DiCaprio for *J.Edgar* and Ryan Gosling for *The Ides Of March*.

The news capped a brilliant year for Michael, who returned home to Fossa just before Christmas to see his family and friends. Josef and Adele had retired from running the West End House restaurant and it was now under new management but, accompanied by his parents, he popped in to say hello to everyone and to pose for some photographs, including one of him pulling a pint of Guinness behind the bar. A large poster of *Hunger*, signed by Michael and the cast, now hangs on one of the walls. Michael also enjoyed a drink with some old friends in The Laurels pub, where he received a lot of good-natured ribbing about *Shame*.

Although Michael was now living in London, he still thought of Ireland as his natural home because it was where he grew up. He still feels comfortable there, so he usually returns three times a year. Christmas time and Easter – he and Josef have birthdays in April – are two periods he aims for. And he can always expect some mickey-taking from his family and friends over his diluted Irish accent.

Early in January 2012 Michael, rather jaded from the treadmill of movie publicity and the revelries of the Christmas and New Year festivities, flew to the Hawaiian island of Oahu for some fresh air. And being the thrill seeker he is, he felt the best way to do this was to parachute from a plane. He was strapped to the instructor as the plane flew over the island and after they jumped out they free-fell for 50 seconds, which he later described as 'the most amazing rush. You're free falling and your brain is saying, "What are you doing?" Once the canopy opens, he unhooks certain things and you drop down a bit. It's a crazy feeling to jump out of an airplane and land on the ground.'

The month of January saw his fan base swell when he appeared bare-chested, sitting on a bed, on the cover of the *Hollywood Reporter*. Then it was back to the round of awards ceremonies and movie publicity and more personal accolades as he had to make even more room on his shelves for awards.

The National Board of Review Awards at the Cipriani, 42nd Street in New York, attracted the cream of showbiz talent, including George Clooney, Martin Scorsese, Emma Stone, Helen Mirren, Keira Knightley and Daniel Radcliffe. At the ceremonies, Scorsese's animated children's film *Hugo*, about an orphaned boy living in Paris, was named Best Film and he also picked up Best Director. In a standout year for George Clooney, he was awarded Best Actor, with Tilda Swinton winning Best Actress and Christopher Plummer Best Supporting Actor.

The Spotlight award, honouring the year's most prolific actor, went to Michael, who was presented with his trophy by his co-stars Keira Knightley and Carey Mulligan. From the stage, Keira addressed Michael in the audience with the comment, 'If I had to be spanked by anybody, I'm glad it was by you.' And Carey remarked that the most-used adjective to describe Michael's work over the past year had been 'fearless'.

In his acceptance speech, Michael humbly said that he always felt like an interloper at events like this. By now used to jokes about his nudity, he added, 'I had to bare all in order to get here. When all else fails, I take my clothes off.'

Next up was the Los Angeles Film Critics Association Awards at the InterContinental Hotel in Century City, where he won Best Actor for his '2011 Body of Work'. Meanwhile, cinema audiences were getting the chance to see *Shame*. Most critics raved about it in some of the best reviews that the team could have hoped for.

'For Fassbender, it is a brilliant piece of work,' said the *Daily Telegraph*. 'Michael Fassbender and Carey Mulligan give dynamite performances,' said the *Guardian*. 'Completely unself-conscious about the full-frontal nudity and graphically simulated sex acts required of him, the actor peels back layers of lust and self-loathing to become a consummate vessel for the director's intentions,' gushed *Variety*. 'Even when he says nothing, which is most of the time, Fassbender transfixes.'

'Michael Fassbender bares all – and then some – in a riveting performance as a Manhattan sex addict spiralling out of control,' said the *New York Post*. 'Stark, explicit and at times shocking, British director Steve McQueen's powerful and beautifully made drama features a stunning lead performance by actor-of-the-moment Michael Fassbender,' opined the *Sunday Mirror*. 'A powerhouse of a performance from Fassbender,' the *Sun* concurred.

'Michael Fassbender delivers a bold and brilliantly immersive performance as a sex addict in *Shame*. He is so raw and riveting you won't be able to take your eyes off him,' said *Rolling Stone*. 'Fassbender is the full package in a carnal drama that spares no blushes and pulls no punches,' said *Total Film*.

But some critics were put off by the subject matter and seediness of it all. '*Shame* is a giant yawn that proves once again that sex as a cinematic subject is one colossal turn-off,' asserted the *Daily Express*. Its fellow 'middle England' newspaper, the *Daily Mail*, also swam against the tide: 'While *Shame* has style to spare, it isn't as well-written, entertaining, or as socially and sexually aware as it pretends to be.'

Having flown to LA for The Golden Globes, Michael was delighted to spot fellow Irishman Brendan Gleeson on the red carpet. The two actors warmly embraced each other and posed for photographs as the guests made their way into the Beverly Hilton for the event, hosted for the second year running by Ricky Gervais.

The silent black and white film, *The Artist*, had received the greatest number of nominations – six – and scooped three awards on the night – Best Film (Musical or Comedy), Best Actor (for its French star Jean Dujardin) and Best Score. It was now hotly tipped for Oscar success the following month.

The Descendents, starring George Clooney as a Hawaiian lawyer attempting to reconnect with his daughters, was named Best Film (Drama) and George also pipped Michael to the Best Actor (Drama) award. But in his acceptance speech George put Michael in the spotlight with a jokey reference to *Shame*. 'I would like to thank Michael Fassbender for taking over the frontal nude responsibly that I had,' he quipped, to much amusement from the audience. 'Really, Michael, honestly, you can play golf like this with your hands behind your back,' he continued, rocking from side to side with his hands behind him. 'Go for it, man. Do it!'

At the Fox after-party, where the studio boss Rupert Murdoch held court, Michael puffed on a giant cigar. But talk of a possible Oscar nomination made him fidgety. 'It would just be a bonus but of course I would take my mom down the red carpet,' he said with a smile.

January 2012 also saw the release of *Haywire,* which encountered mixed reviews. Some were happy just to sit back and soak up the kick-ass action from Gina Carano but others thought it lacked the punch of, for example, the *Bourne* movies. With Gina the undoubted star of the movie – Michael having made only a relatively brief if crucial appearance – she received most of the attention.

Most reviews agreed that the movie passed the action test. 'This isn't just the best action film since *Bourne*, it also exudes the sort of flair and cool of a 1960s Bond movie. A class act,' enthused the *Daily Mirror*. 'A breathless, bone-crunching espionage thriller distinguished by its female protagonist, Mallory Kane, played by mixed-martial-arts star Gina Carano,' said the *Daily Express*.

Thereafter praise seemed to concentrate on the director's particular style. 'Steven Soderbergh has mashed, fermented and distilled a range of familiar [1970s] revenge-movie tropes into a cask-strength action thriller,' said the *Daily Telegraph*. 'Only Steven Soderbergh could produce a slick, modern, cine-literate deconstruction of the Hollywood action caper that also manages to be a rollicking good ride,' claimed *Time Out London*. 'A fresh, muscular payback movie shot through with Soderbergh's mischievous indie-spirit,' was *Empire*'s take.

The meandering plot, however, was a niggling concern. 'Gina Carano is great beating up her co-stars but Steven Soderbergh's thriller is a bit boring in-between,' said the *Guardian*. '*Haywire* just isn't thrilling,' agreed the *Daily Mail*. 'Less a tightly plotted action film than an excuse to showcase Carano's substantial fighting skills,' thought the *Los Angeles Times*. 'A vigorous spy thriller that consistently beckons the viewer to catch up with its narrative twists and turns. Bordering on convoluted, it works best when in combat mode,' said *USA Today*.

In the end qualified praise seemed to be the overall verdict. 'Hard, fast, brutal: Soderbergh's sucker-punch return to action knows what it's about. Not subtle or substantial but it gets to work with flab-free focus,' stated *Total Film*. 'A film like *Haywire* has no lasting significance but it's a pleasure to see an A-list director taking the care to make a first-rate genre thriller,' opined the *Chicago Sun-Times*.

With the awards season still in full flow, it was back to London for the next one – the London Film Critics Circle Awards at The British Film Institute. Here Michael received yet another trophy – this time for British Actor of the Year – but there was criticism from some Irish newspapers that their talented actor was considered British. When asked about this, Michael light-heartedly dismissed the issue with the comment, 'When I make a shit film, no one will want to claim me!'

He also joked about being naked in *Shame* and *Hunger*. 'From the start of my career, I've been naked. My first job was a commercial for SAS airlines. I wake up in a pink room next to a beautiful blonde girl and get out of bed naked. From that point forward, it's been in all of my contracts: "He must be naked in this film."'

Having won so many awards and been feted around the world, Michael and his colleagues took a deep breath as the nominations for the Academy Awards were announced at the end of January. Despite trying not to think about it, this was the big one. The ultimate accolade. The stuff of dreams.

The excitement and anxiety were heightened the day before nominations were due to be announced when hotly tipped Michael was invited to *Newsweek* magazine's traditional 'Oscar Roundtable' chat, in which a handful of likely nominees sit around a table and are asked questions by their host. An informal occasion, it's more akin to an A-list dinner party. Joining Michael were George Clooney, Charlize Theron, Christopher Plummer, Tilda Swinton and Viola Davis. Often the actors have not met before but this year's gathering had a lot of shared history. George Clooney and Viola Davis had worked together on *Solaris* a decade ago and he had lent her his Lake Como villa for her honeymoon. He was also friends with Tilda Swinton, having bonded on the films *Michael Clayton* and *Burn After Reading*. And Michael and Charlize had spent months together shooting *Prometheus*.

In high spirits, Michael popped out just before the photo-shoot with a publicist and returned with a bottle of vodka and a Bloody Mary mix. In a throwback to his bartender days, he set up an impromptu bar in the green room, pouring drinks for everybody despite it being well before noon. (Incidentally he can also mix up a fine vodka martini.) Michael and George then threw themselves into a boisterous game of table-tennis and had to be encouraged away for the round-table conversation to begin.

During the course of the conversation there was much light-hearted banter, led by George, who continually teased Michael about his penis, suggesting that it would make an ideal centrepiece for the table! And in a discussion about the rules governing the showing of on-screen erections, George halted Tilda and gestured towards Michael, saying, 'Let's go to the pro.' This prompted Michael to proclaim that he had 'peed on cue' during *Shame*, which he hadn't been sure he'd be able to do.

When the topic moved on to trailers, Michael told how impressed he'd been the first time he had a big trailer on a movie location. George felt that some actors were vain in demanding big trailers but Tilda argued that she thought they were for the protection of actors and that it was not, 'Oooh, I've got a big trailer, then I must have a big cock.' Quick as a flash, Charlize quipped, 'Leave him out of this,' glancing at Michael. 'There are exceptions,' he replied, turning red.

A few days earlier, Michael had been asked by *Total Film* magazine if he thought that the Academy would be brave enough to give an award to something as challenging as *Shame*. 'That's not really my concern,' he replied.

I'd be lying to say that it wouldn't be nice to get an Oscar. I would be flattered and honoured. But for me to sit down and start thinking about it... there's no benefit to that, there's not a lot I can do with that information. Let's just see what happens. For me, what's really more encouraging and flattering and makes me feel, 'Wow, thank God!' is to see the response of the public and journalists.

It's encouraging because it's the argument I always have about how there are intelligent audiences out there who are willing to be challenged and don't shy away from things that are uncomfortable at times to watch. When I hear people say, I don't know if an audience is ready to accept that or see that, it's like, how the fuck do you know? That's what is really nice about it. The rest, the awards... let's see what happens. Everything after that is a bonus.

Michael's 'que sera, sera' attitude was to serve him well when the nominations were finally announced.

CHAPTER EIGHTEEN

CEREMONY SEASON

To the great surprise of many, Michael and *Shame* failed to make the list of nominees for the Oscars. But Michael's omission in the Best Actor category wasn't the only shock. His fellow Golden Globe nominees Leonardo DiCaprio and Ryan Gosling were also left out, and so was Tilda Swinton for Best Actress.

At the London premiere of *Shame*, Michael was asked about missing out on an Oscar nomination. 'Well, of course there's always a moment where you're like, "Oh shit," but I'm living a pretty charmed life,' he said. 'A statue is nice but the fact that I get to work with so many talented people is much more amazing and nourishing for me.'

Steve McQueen was more irritated though and more outspoken. 'In America they're too scared of sex – that's why he [Michael] wasn't nominated,' he insisted. 'If you look at the Best Actor list you're saying, "Michael Fassbender is not on that list?" It's kind of crazy. But that's how it is. It's an American award, let them have it.'

He wasn't alone in his opinion of the Academy being put off by the subject matter of *Shame* – several film critics agreed with him. But it was *The Artist* that charmed the Academy and on the night scooped a total of five awards including Best Film, Best Actor for Jean Dujardin and Best Director.

A few days before the Oscar nominations were announced, Michael attended a Q&A for *Shame* at his local cinema, the Hackney Picture House, where he was questioned on stage by the film editor of *Time Out* magazine, Dave Calhoun. Those present were given some interesting insights into Michael and the way he worked. When he was asked about his rush of films – *Inglourious Basterds, X-Men: First Class, Jane Eyre, A Dangerous Method* and *Haywire* – he grinned and, paraphrasing washed-up actor Troy McClure from *The Simpsons*, he replied, 'It reminds me of *The Simpsons*, "Hi, I'm Troy McClure, you might have seen me in..."'

He also explained the way that he approached an acting role. For a man who likes to be fully prepared – reading and re-reading a script up to 300 times – when it came to the actual acting, he didn't like things too planned.

'That's boring. You want to prepare yourself and then be able to react, be awake, be aware and that's when you're really cooking,' he said. 'It's like music and you are jamming as opposed to rolling out a very polished set. It's like an album. You go into a studio and you have to do something within a restricted time. It doesn't give you the time to polish it. It might not be a perfect piece but the essence of it is something really interesting. The rawness of it and the electricity.'

Despite his consuming passion for his work, Michael has always been a very down-to-earth person and aware of the dangers of being perceived as pretentious and a bore. So he makes sure that he shakes off his roles at the end of a day's filming. 'When you're meeting other people you don't want them thinking, "Oh, here goes Mike again, talking about his characters,"' he said.

At the end of January, he attended the UK Gala Premiere of *A Dangerous Method* at the Mayfair Hotel in London with Keira Knightley and Viggo Mortensen. At the after-show party, he really let his hair down. Dancing with Keira, he bent her over backwards as he hammed it up on the dance floor. Later he played the piano and even danced with Viggo, grinning and laughing, before being carried out on the back of one of the guests to a waiting taxi – the *Sun* later splashed pictures of him in high spirits.

Reviews for *A Dangerous Method* were generally good, although a common theme was that it was a little plodding. Most enthusiastic was the *Hollywood Reporter*, which gushed, 'Precise, lucid and thrillingly disciplined, this story of boundary-testing in the early days of psychoanalysis is brought to vivid life by the outstanding lead performances of Keira Knightley, Viggo Mortensen and Michael Fassbender.' To the *Observer* it was 'engrossing, admirably acted', while the *Independent* said, 'The film boasts two assured performances from Michael Fassbender and Viggo Mortensen and a very brave, if uneven one, from Keira Knightley in her most challenging role to date.'

The *Guardian*, however, thought the film 'heavy and lugubrious. It is a tale that comes marinated in port and choked on pipe-smoke. You long for it to hop down from the couch, throw open the windows and run about in the garden.' The *Daily Telegraph* also thought it lacked pace: 'What's odd, for Cronenberg, is how the film can feel like an advert for buttoned-down restraint rather than danger or release. Spotlessly organised, it's an exercise the director knows he can pull off without breaking a sweat.' *Empire* magazine said, 'It never really gets under the skin in the way Cronenberg does at his best.'

The *Toronto Star* had a different take. It liked the slow pace of the movie, saying, 'Cronenberg has reached the stage of his career where he doesn't feel it necessary to pander to expectations. Instead he seeks to engage us, and he succeeds.' The *Seattle Times* concurred that it was 'an elegant, almost stately film, with the emphasis on ideas and discussion rather than dramatic action'. The *Los*

Angeles Times, too, enjoyed the understated acting between the two male leads – 'It's fascinating to see the exceptionally charismatic Fassbender squeeze himself into the role of the aristocratic, restrained Jung, and it's just as enjoyable to see Mortensen bring an unexpected virility to his sybaritic, cigar-chomping Freud.'

In February Michael was voted Best Actor for *Shame* at the *Evening Standard* British Film Awards. (He didn't attend the ceremony so Abi Morgan accepted the award in his place.) And Michael was definitely man of the month as far as the glossy magazines were concerned, appearing on the cover of *GQ*, *Interview* and the Singapore men's style magazine *August Man*, and being pictured naked in bed with a sheet covering his modesty for *W* magazine.

Touching on his own view of personal relationships, he admitted to *Marie Claire* magazine that he found them difficult to pursue because of his work. 'To be honest, relationships as a whole for me in this industry have been a difficult thing to maintain,' he said, 'It goes with the territory. I would be prepared to walk away from relationships because of my job. I wanted to give this everything and go for it 110 per cent, so I guess my work has taken precedence over that.'

On the same subject, he was equally honest with *OK!* magazine: 'It's very difficult to maintain a relationship doing this kind of job. I know people do manage to maintain marriages and relationships within it, but I'm pretty selfish in terms of how I work and the time I take.

'I would want to give my all to a relationship if I did find the right woman but I rarely even get to spend time with friends and family and would struggle to fully commit. I disappear, I don't see my friends for like four weeks or very seldom I see them, so it's not fair on a partner when you're not there and investing and giving them something to sort of work with. At the moment, I'm concentrating on work.'

On a more positive note he added that he doesn't 'close himself off to love' and thought that it was a wonderful thing. 'If you fall in love, you've got to go with it because it's an amazing journey. One person can do something, two people together can experience things together – it's much more beautiful to share.'

For those taking notes, he also talked about the parts of a woman's body that he found particularly attractive – the neck, shoulders, hands and wrists.

A few days later it was a weekend of award ceremonies. First he travelled to Dublin where he enjoyed a meal in the Chop House restaurant with some friends on the Friday night before attending the IFTAs at the Dublin Convention Centre the following day, where he scooped the Best Actor award for *Shame*.

In the morning it was a quick flight back to London with his parents, who were accompanying him to the BAFTAs. Here Michael was competing with Leonardo DiCaprio, Gary Oldman, Brad Pitt, George Clooney and Jean Dujardin in the Best Actor category. Dujardin won and *Shame* lost out to *Tinker Tailor Soldier Spy* for Outstanding

British Film but Michael couldn't have been more delighted when *Pitch Black Heist* was announced as Best Short Film, heartily applauding John Maclean as he made his way to the stage.

Outside on the red carpet, Michael told reporters that John was writing a feature film that he would appear in. When John was asked about why Michael wanted to work with him, he joked, 'He's so talented he can work like this on many different levels. Tarantino at the top, Steve McQueen one level down and me right at the very bottom!' Michael then took Josef and Adele with him to the after-show party – and this time he was on his best behaviour!

With the awards season in full swing, a week later he was in Germany for the Berlin International Film Festival where *Haywire* was premiered and the fight scenes were greeted with much whooping and cheering.

In his early years Michael had laid down a steady body of work in which he had applied himself to learning his craft. Despite his phenomenal success and the attendant acclaim that followed his breakthrough with *Hunger*, memories of the lean times are never far from his mind. He had wondered then whether he would ever make it and he remains level-headed now about stardom. He enjoys his time in the spotlight but he is aware that there is always a 'new boy' lurking in the shadows, waiting to take his place.

'Nothing changes. My life continues how it is. It really is that simple,' he told the London newspaper *Metro*. 'All this other stuff... it's kind of like the hula hoop. You know the hula hoop comes into fashion and everybody's doing the hula hoop and three years later it's that bouncing space hopper or the skateboard. So at the moment, a sort of amount of attention comes my way but it is what it is.'

Towards the end of 2011, Michael and screenwriter Ronan Bennett (best known for 2009's *Public Enemies*) had been working on an idea to make a film about the mythical eighth-century Celtic hero, Cuchulain. By February 2012, they had managed to raise the finance through their new production company Finn McCool Films. Fittingly, the company was named after another mighty figure from Irish legend, a 52ft tall giant who threw stones and turf into the sea while fighting the Scottish giant Benandonnar – thereby creating the famous Giant's Causeway of hexagonal basalt columns.

Cuchulain is the central character in the *Ulster Cycle*, an epic series of Old Irish legends which tells the saga of the Ulaid tribe headed by King Conchobar and their battles against the invading Connachta tribe from the south, led by Queen Mebh. The most prominent figure in the legends is Conchobar's nephew Cuchulain, a fearsome warrior with fantastic fighting skills. In the most famous story, *The Cattle Raid of Cooley*, Mebh sends her vast army to steal Conchobar's prize white bull. After the Ulaid have been disabled by a curse, 17-year-old

Cuchulain finds himself the only one capable of resistance. He invokes the right of single combat at fords and defeats the warriors one by one until he has to face his foster brother and best friend, Ferdiad. After four days of struggle Cuchulain eventually triumphs but is filled with remorse for having killed Ferdiad.

Cuchulain's favoured means of transport was the chariot but Michael opted for a more modern version of horsepower when he was invited to appear on the BBC motoring show *Top Gear*. His love of speed and Formula 1 meant that he was asked to take part in one of the most enjoyable segments of the show, called Star in a Reasonably Priced Car. This involves a celebrity driving as fast as they can around a track in an average car, with their speed put on a board ranking the fastest to the lowest. Past celebrities to have taken part included Tom Cruise and Cameron Diaz.

The host, Jeremy Clarkson, introduced Michael to the show by saying he was half Irish, half German – 'so top o' the morgen to Michael Fassbender.' Michael was not the only excited person in the studio. Jeremy revealed that in all the years he had been hosting *Top Gear*, only a handful of his friends had asked for tickets to the show. But when Michael was due on, he had been besieged by people wanting tickets and had to hire a mini-bus to transport a crowd of girls!

Jeremy was surprised to learn that his guest had only owned one car in his life – a Peugeot 306, turbo-diesel

Spinnaker, special edition – which he had crashed. In the early part of the show, Michael got to drive a McLaren racing car around a track. Then it was time for Star in a Reasonably Priced Car, for which he was given a Kia. Driving it was made more difficult because ice had formed on part of the track and, although most of it had been dug away, some remained on one corner.

During his drive, shown in the studio on a screen, he had everyone laughing as he sat, tense and determined in the driving seat muttering, 'I'm sweating like a cornered nun.' After he was seen crossing the finishing line, Jeremy asked him how he thought he did. Michael said he would have been happy with 1 minute, 45 seconds but he didn't think he would get that. On the leader board he could see the likes of Tom Cruise on 1.44.2, Nick Frost on 1.44.5, Simon Pegg on 144.9, Cameron Diaz on 145.2, Rupert Grint on 1.45.5 and Boris Becker on 145.9.

When Jeremy announced that he had done it in 1.42.8, Michael was shocked. The audience applauded wildly as Jeremy informed him that it was the third fastest time ever and put him just behind leader Matt Le Blanc on 1.42.1 and Rowan Atkinson on 142.2.

Having taken a break from making back-to-back movies, Michael was now eager to get working again. He had been in early discussions with Ridley Scott to star in his new movie, *The Counselor*, playing a successful lawyer who ends up in a desperate situation after dabbling in the drug business. The screenplay was by Cormac McCarthy, writer of the acclaimed *No Country for Old Men*, *The Road* and *All the Pretty Horses*. The film's producer, Steven Schwartz, explained that the story was set in a masculine world into which two women intrude to play leading roles. Michael signed up to the film in February, with filming due to start in May.

In the meantime, he had also agreed to team up for the third time with Steve McQueen for his new movie, *Twelve Years a Slave*. It was an adaptation of Solomon Northup's 1853 book about his time as a freeborn man of mixed race who, in 1841, was lured from New York to Washington – then a slave-owning district – with the promise of a well-paid job playing his fiddle in a circus. He was then drugged and awoke to find himself in a slave pen and subsequently lived under a number of owners, enduring great hardship. While toiling on a cotton plantation in Louisiana he confided his story to a white farmer from Canada named Samuel Bass, who had arrived to do some work there. Solomon realised that Samuel disagreed with the treatment of slaves and persuaded him to deliver a letter to his wife back home in New York, telling her what had happened and where he was. She then went to court to try to free him and finally succeeded in 1853.

Steve had co-written the screenplay with John Ridley, a novelist (his first, *Stray Dogs*, had been turned into the 1997 movie *U-Turn* by Oliver Stone) and screenwriter of the 2002 comedy movie, *Undercover Brother*, and the film was to be produced by Brad Pitt.

Michael was also in talks to be in Brendan Gleeson's debut movie, *At Swim Two-Birds*, a film adaptation of the acclaimed 1939 novel by Irish writer Brian O'Nolan under the pseudonym Flann O'Brien. (Gabriel Byrne, Colin Farrell and Cillian Murphy were also in discussions.) The complex plot of this witty novel concerns a lazy and frequently drunk student who lives with his uncle in Dublin, where he is writing – mostly from his bed – a novel about Dermot Trellis, the proprietor of a Dublin pub, who in turn is writing a novel. But Trellis is also lazy and asleep for much of the time and the characters from his novel rebel against him and ultimately the unnamed student. The characters include a polite devil, a posse of cowboys and the ancient Irish giant Finn McCool.

Michael talked it over with Brendan over a meal at the Chop House restaurant in Dublin but they were interrupted when it was brought to their attention that it was a special night for one girl in the room, as it was her birthday. Both of them went over to her table to express their best wishes and happily posed for pictures with her.

Because he knows what it is like trying to make it as an actor and is appreciative of those who helped and encouraged him, Michael has always been keen to do the same with new talent. It was no big surprise, therefore, that he agreed to become part of the Your Film Festival team, for a competition organised by YouTube and others (including Ridley Scott) to find the world's best storytellers and connect them with a global audience. Ten finalists, chosen by the viewing public, would attend the Venice Film Festival in 2012 where the winner of grand prize would receive $500,000 (£315,000) to work on their next project.

Submissions opened at the beginning of February 2012 and Michael committed himself to joining Ridley Scott as a juror, as well as being co-executive producer on the winning project. 'When you are trying to make it within this industry – to get your films seen – you just really have to go out there and do it,' he said. 'Ridley Scott told me that the first time he directed he had a [instruction] book in one hand and a camera in the other. By doing things you learn.'

The following month Michael embarked on talks about starring in another movie – a romantic adventure called *The Mountain Between Us*, based on the book by Charles Martin and to be directed by Gerardo Naranjo, who had helmed the Mexican thriller, *Miss Bala*.

It tells the story of a stormy night when passengers are stranded at Salt Lake City airport after commercial flights are cancelled due to dangerous flying conditions. Doctor and keen climber Ben Payne, who has been attending a medical conference, manages to charter a private plane that will take him around the storm and drop him in Denver to catch a connecting flight home to Jacksonville, Florida. Touched by the anxieties of attractive and successful writer Ashley Knox, who is desperate to get home for her wedding, he offers her a seat in the plane. She gratefully accepts but the unthinkable happens when the elderly pilot has a heart attack over the desolate mountainous wasteland of the High Uintas Wilderness in Utah.

Ben manages to crash-land and, although they survive, they are badly injured. He has broken ribs and possibly a collapsed lung and Ashley suffers a dislocated shoulder, a broken leg and probable internal injuries. Fortunately, Ben has his mountaineering equipment with him but first he needs to nurse Ashley back to health. With little food and freezing conditions, time is running out. Meanwhile, Ashley realises that the very private Ben has some serious emotional issues. Another realisation comes a little later – she may be falling in love with him.

But it was Michael's off-screen love life that became public news. In March he was pictured walking around the Soho district in New York with his arm around what the newspapers and several websites at first described as a 'mystery woman' until she was identified as Nicole Beharie. As usual, Michael would not comment publicly on their relationship but it was clear from their body language that they were more than 'just good friends'.

In the June issue of *GQ*, however, he was a little more forthcoming. 'I'm seeing Nicole, we're trying to see each other as often as possible,' he confirmed. 'That's kind of difficult when she lives [in New York] and I live in England.

Nothing happened while we were filming,' he added. 'We started talking more on the promotion thing. So, yeah, it just sort of unfolded like that.'

CHAPTER NINETEEN

MAN OF THE YEAR?

In March the progress of *Prometheus* – with its release due less than three months away on 8 June – was causing much excitement. Most of the story had been successfully kept under wraps but a new trailer at the annual comic-book and science convention WonderCon hinted at what was to come.

Some of the main cast members, including Michael and Charlize Theron, along with director Ridley Scott and writer Damon Lindelof, attended the convention in Anaheim, California. There had been much speculation about whether this was actually a prequel of *Alien* or a totally different story and Damon went some way to putting the record straight. '*Prometheu*s isn't a prequel because it doesn't end when *Alien* begins,' he said. 'This word "prequel" was on the table. It was the elephant in the room and had to be discussed. If there were a sequel to this movie [*Prometheus*], it would not be *Alien*. Normally, that's the definition of a prequel – it precedes the other movies.

'This movie,' he added, 'hopefully will contextualize the original *Alien* so that when you watch it again, maybe you know a little bit more, but you don't fuck around with that movie. It has to stand on its own. It's a classic. But if we're fortunate enough to do a sequel to *Prometheus*, it will actually, I think, tangentalise even further away from the original *Alien*.'

Following the press conference, Michael and Charlize took part in a Q&A session in which they answered questions about the film emailed to them from around the world. Their growing friendship meant they were comfortable teasing each other and it was an entertaining session.

Michael told how he was fascinated by the philosophy behind the script – the beginnings of mankind, why we are all here, who created us and what happens to us when we die. He also reiterated that he based David's physicality on the American Olympic diver, Greg Louganis. 'I always remember him walking towards the edge of the diving board and I thought it was a very neutral and practical position, so that was the launching pad.' He also described Ridley as being 'quite a mischievous character with a childish energy which is infectious to be around'.

Charlize got the last laugh when answering the final question: if one day a spaceship came to Earth with aliens, what would you really do? 'I think it's already happened. Half the people in this room are freakin' aliens,' she replied, then gestured towards Michael.

A few days later and Michael was reunited with Charlize when he presented her with an Ally for Equality Award at the Human Rights Campaign gala in Los Angeles. She was being honoured for her work with the lesbian, gay, bisexual and transgender community. Once more Michael's penis was the subject for humour! In her acceptance speech, Charlize turned towards Michael and, referring to his full frontal exploits in *Shame*, said, 'I have to say that I was truly impressed that you chose to play it big. Most other actors would have gone small, trust me. No, I know because I've worked with them.' She went on to lift her glass for a toast and added, 'Your penis was a revelation. I'm available to work with it any time.'

The film world's love affair with Michael continued as he picked up no less than a Hero Award at the Jameson Empire Film Awards, held at London's Grosvenor Hotel. Stars attending included Danny DeVito, Ron Howard, Tim Burton, Dolph Lundgren, Morgan Spurlock, Gary Oldman, Agyness Deyn, Tom Hiddleston, Olivia Wilde, Chris Hemsworth and David Morrissey. It was a good night for Gary Oldman, who was voted Best Actor, with *Tinker Tailor Soldier Spy* acclaimed as Best British Film and Best Thriller.

Towards the end of the evening came the special awards. Director Ron Howard won the Empire Inspiration award, then screenwriter Jane Goldman (of *Kick-Ass* fame) walked on to present Michael with his Hero award. 'The winner this year has often been described as sex on legs but, as it happens, he also has intelligence, charm, passion and vulnerability on legs as well,' she said. 'Film has always been his passion – he appeared in a stage version of *Reservoir Dogs* fourteen years ago; since then he's appeared in a Tarantino film. Whatever the genre, he grounds his characters in reality. He lost three stone in *Hunger*, he spanked Keira Knightley in *A Dangerous Method* and in *Shame* he bared all. But in each case he transcends actorly stunts. But perhaps his greatest performance of the last twelve months is the patience he's shown in the face of continual questions from journalists about his physical assets.'

Michael looked a little bit embarrassed at being labelled 'a hero' but it put a big smile on his face. Accepting the award, he commented, 'Well, this is kind of unusual because the first job I wanted to do was to be Superman, so a hero award is official now, thanks to *Empire*. It's a magazine I actually always did read and follow as a film fan. And Jameson is my favourite whiskey, so this is pretty special!'

But the jokes about Michael's 'assets' weren't over yet. For the finale Danny DeVito took to the stage to announce Tim Burton as Empire Icon. 'Tim and I did three movies together; the last one was *Big Fish*,' he said. 'I owned a circus and I was a werewolf, and that was really fun. It was the first movie where you got to see my ass on screen. He said, "There's gonna be a shot of the back of you." You don't realise there are going to be ninety people watching. That would've been embarrassing but I borrowed Fassbender's schlong so that was OK.'

Afterwards, when asked by a reporter who his own personal heroes were, Michael commented, 'There are a lot of heroes out there. People who are sacrificing their lives to try to improve other people's lives.'

Despite all the mickey-taking about his public nudity, Michael brazened it out with yet more exposure! That month he caused a stir among his fans when he was the cover star for the glossy French magazine *Obsession*. Inside was a picture of him half-naked, removing his jeans while displaying a muscular torso. Another photograph showed a side view of him, walking completely naked.

In the accompanying article, Michael modestly told the magazine that whenever he was sent a film script he thought of 10 other actors who would be better in it than him but were not fortunate enough to be sent such material. He also reiterated his compulsion to challenge himself as an actor and to surprise others. 'My biggest mistake would be to let the industry put a label on me, so I do things unexpected – not suicidal, because I want all this to continue and develop – but it's good to take risks.'

Michael was also on the cover of the German magazine

Arte in April and then found himself on *Time* magazine's prestigious annual list of the 100 most influential people 'who most affect our world'. His citation stated that it had been a 'huge year' for him 'mixing mainstream fare (*X Men: First Class*) with independent cinema (*Jane Eyre, A Dangerous Method* and *Shame*)'.

AFTERWORD

Ａnd what of the future? The principles Michael has lived by so far – taking chances and appreciating his good fortune in getting where he is today – remain his guiding lights.

'I don't take anything for granted and I don't presume that because today is going a certain way tomorrow will be the same,' he says. 'That's something I learned from the times that I wasn't in the position to be allowed to work. When you really feel like this is your job but you have to do something else because you're unemployed in the one you really want to do, it makes you appreciate things and realise how precious it is.'

Michael plans to develop his production company in

order to create his own projects and also to help encourage new talent – be it actors, writers or directors. 'I do think that my job has a shelf life, so maybe I'd like to stop doing this [acting] at some point and look at developing things or working as a director if I feel like I'm equipped enough and I have an interesting enough story to tell.'

But he still has plenty of acting ambitions left. These include being in a Coen brothers film (*The Big Lebowski* is one of his favourites), doing some theatre and one wish in particular which raises an intriguing prospe: 'I'd like to do a musical, at the right time with the right material. Actually, I do have an idea, so maybe I'll develop it myself!'

However, he doesn't fret about what he hasn't done. He only ever wanted to be a jobbing actor, so the rest has been a bonus. 'This whole experience is crazy. When I decided this [acting] was what I wanted to do, this was the situation I dreamed about being in. It's nuts.

'It's incredible to think of the people I have worked with. I often think that I am going to wake up and it's all been a dream. I'm pinching myself quite a lot these days. Touch wood I am allowed to continue to keep learning from these great people. I don't want to spend too much time thinking about the things I've done, or linger in the past. I can find that depressing. The main thing is thinking about what I can do next and making sure I do a good job.'

Michael's rise to stardom has been a triumph of belief, focus, hard work and the vital knack of being able to seize the moment and not letting go. Even in the most difficult times when he was barely surviving in London, he had to face the fact that it might never happen, but still he held onto his dream.

'I trusted myself from the start and I just believed,' he says. 'I kept knocking at the door and at some point there was a crack and I got my toe in. Once I got my toe in, I got the rest of my foot in and the next thing, I was in the room.'